BIRDWATCHING

BY
Eileen Buckle

ILLUSTRATED BY
Jim Robins

MACDONALD

©Macdonald Educational 1979

Adapted and published in
the United States by
Silver Burdett Company,
Morristown, N.J.
1980 Printing

ISBN 0-382-06442-9
Library of Congress
Catalog Card No. 80-50946

Contents

This book has been carefully planned to help you become an expert. Look for the special pages to find the information you need. **RECOGNITION** pages, with a **violet flash** in the top right-hand corner, contain all the essential information to know and remember. **PROJECT** pages, with a **grey border**, suggest some interesting ideas for things to do and make. At the end of the book there is a useful **REFERENCE** section.

Birdwatching as a hobby

Most people like watching birds; they are such lively, attractive creatures. But remember, birdwatching needs plenty of patience. Birds take fright easily when approached. Don't be discouraged. Get to know the more common birds first. Later on you will spot less common species. One of the best things about birdwatching is that you never stop learning.

The science of birdwatching

Many people go birdwatching purely for enjoyment; but keen birdwatchers can play a vital role in the science of birdwatching (ornithology). Bird scientists depend on amateurs for their facts – for example, about when and where particular species have been sighted. If you keep your eyes open, you will be well on the way to becoming an expert.

A feather in your cap if you spot this rare hoopoe.

An anxious thrush on her nest.

Collecting eggs

It is against the law to collect the eggs of most birds today. Birds have a hard enough time surviving as it is, and rarer species are in danger of disappearing altogether.

Protecting birds

If a bird nests in your garden, leave it alone as much as possible. Put back any vegetation you have pulled aside when looking at the nest; an uncovered nest will attract predators.

Never photograph the nests of rare birds. Also be careful not to frighten away the mother bird. If she leaves the nest for too long, the eggs will grow cold.

Remember that the well camouflaged eggs of ground-nesting birds are easy to step on, so be careful when out walking. Also, if birds are frightened away from their nests in seabird colonies, gulls may eat their eggs or chicks.

Birdwatching equipment

No special equipment is necessary to watch and enjoy birds. But you will find that a field guide, a notebook and a good pair of binoculars will help you to get much more out of your hobby. Take care in choosing these and other items of your equipment.

Binoculars

Binoculars vary in weight, magnification, shape and size, as well as in price. So if you plan to buy a pair make sure you get the advice of someone who knows a lot about them, as not all models are suitable for birdwatching.

Choose a pair that are focused by a **central wheel**, and make sure that they are **light** enough to carry around all day.

Classification

Binoculars are classified by two numbers, for example, 10×50. The first number tells you how many times what you are looking at is magnified (10). The second is the diameter in millimetres of the object lens (50). Divide the second figure by the first and you have the 'light-gathering power' – in this case 5.

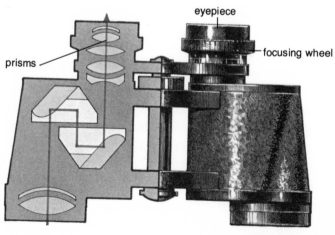

eyepiece

focusing wheel

prisms

object lens

Choosing binoculars

A high light-gathering power makes it easier to see birds in poor light but it also makes the binoculars heavy and more difficult to balance. This is because they need a larger object lens. For all-round birdwatching, 8×30 or 9×35 binoculars are probably the most suitable. Try and buy the best pair that you can afford – perhaps a good second-hand pair.

Telescope

A telescope is really a luxury. It can be useful in a hide, or for watching seabirds at long range, but it is heavy and needs a firm support. Also it is difficult to pinpoint flying birds without a lot of practice as it has a very small 'field of view' (the width of the area you can see).

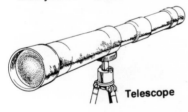

Telescope

Camera

Simple cameras are fine for the more tame garden or park birds, but most birds will not wait for you to get close to them, and any movement will blur your picture. For good bird photography you need a 35mm camera, preferably with a telephoto lens. To choose one, consult a specialist book on wildlife or bird photography *(see page 54).*

Field guide

You will want to identify the birds you see. For this you need a good field guide – with pictures and descriptions of all the birds you are likely to come across. There are several excellent pocket guides available that are easy to carry. Keep other books at home for more detailed reference, or consult them at your local library.

Choose a field guide with a colour picture of a bird on the same page as its description, and a distribution map showing you where you are most likely to see it *(see page 61 for some suggestions).*

Notebook and pencil

These are perhaps the most useful items of equipment.

Choose a notebook with a waterproof backing, or keep it in a plastic case.

black head

dark tail

pink chest

brown wings

size: sparrow or slightly smaller
date: 14th June 3.45 pm
where: gorse bush on cliff side
voice: wheet · tchak -

What to wear

What you wear to go birdwatching depends on both the weather and the type of place you are going to visit. Most birds will see you long before you see them, so try not to attract their attention. Avoid bright colours and stick to the duller tones of brown, grey and dark green.

Summer gear
In summer wear lightweight clothes. You may be walking through rough countryside so make sure that they are fairly tough, or old.

Keeping dry
You can never trust the weather, so always take a light mac with you. If you have a pair of nylon over-trousers use them for walking in long grass after rain or in the early morning dew – the trousers can be rolled up and kept in your pocket when you are not using them.

Carrying your equipment
Your notebook and pencil, a field guide and a map should all fit in the pockets of your mac or anorak. Other things, like an extra jumper, a thermos flask and sandwiches can be carried in a small rucksack. Line it with polythene to keep out the rain. If you are going to be sitting around for long periods, take a blow-up cushion as well – it can make birdwatching much more enjoyable!

SUMMER

WET

lightweight waterproof anorak

DRY

binoculars

light jacket

rucksack
big pocket

camera

nylon over-trousers

jeans or cord trousers

wellingtons

comfortable walking shoes

WINTER

WET   DRY
                    rollneck
                    jumper
                    warm
                    waterproof
                    anorak

              thick
              trousers

              two pairs
              of thick
              socks
wellingtons

              walking boots

Keeping warm

Whatever the season, and particularly in winter, it is as well to be prepared for the cold. The most useful piece of clothing is a warm, weather-proof jacket with lots of deep pockets which either zip or button up. You can keep all the pieces of equipment you need to get at quickly and easily inside.

Footwear

For rough and mountainous country strong walking shoes are best. In marshy areas wear wellingtons, although beware – they can be very tiring on really long walks.

Birdwatching in the cold

If you are a keen birdwatcher the cold won't put you off. But make sure you wrap up warmly. Wear gloves but not thick, clumsy ones that would make it difficult to write notes or focus your binoculars.

thermos flask   waterproof trousers   rucksack
                 and anorak

              notebook   map

field guide   sandwiches

pencil

The bird's habitat

Adapting to the environment

In every type of environment, you will find that the birds there are specially adapted to living and obtaining food in that particular habitat.

Some species may be found in more than one type of habitat as they have quite a varied diet. Others are much more specialized.

Looking at beaks

goldfinch

hawfinch

▲ Seed-eaters.

swallow   skylark

▲ Insect-eaters.

▼ The sparrowhawk's beak can tear at animal flesh.

▼ The beaks of curlew and avocet are designed for sifting mud.

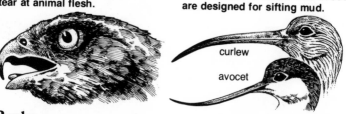

curlew

avocet

Beaks

If a bird has a short, pointed beak then it is mainly an insect-eater. Grain- or seed-eating birds have heavier beaks. Seeds come in all sizes; the stouter the beak, the larger the seeds it can tackle. The goldfinch eats small thistle seeds with its slender beak. The much larger beak of the hawfinch can crack open a cherry stone.

Feet and legs

A bird's foot usually has four toes, three pointing forward and one backwards. When perching, the hind toe curls over to meet the front three. The woodpecker, a tree-climber, needs a very firm grip so it has two of its toes pointing forward and two backwards. The swift has all four toes pointing forward; it spends most of its time in the air.

The long legs of wading birds enable them to search for food in shallow waters. Most waders also have long toes, spread wide for walking on mud. Moorhens, coots and mallards share the same habitat, but have different feet depending on how long they spend on land and in the water.

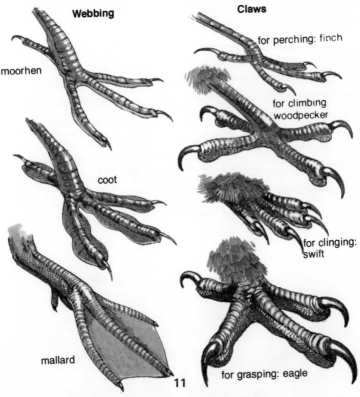

Webbing

Claws

moorhen

coot

mallard

for perching: finch

for climbing: woodpecker

for clinging: swift

for grasping: eagle

Birdwatching in towns

Towns may not seem like good places to go birdwatching. But large numbers of birds make their homes there. Even in very built-up areas you will be able to spot town or 'feral' pigeons, and house sparrows nesting on ledges and under eaves. They usually feed on bread and scraps but sometimes also eat seeds and grain.

In the city centre

Starlings flock into many large cities to roost at night. During the day they search nearby gardens and parks for insects, seeds and berries.

High up in the sky you may see a kestrel hovering. Many have moved into towns in recent years. They feed on sparrows, mice and beetles. During late spring and early summer, swifts and house martins can be seen wheeling about over rooftops. They are catching flying insects.

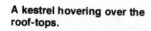

A kestrel hovering over the roof-tops.

Starlings coming home to roost.

In parks and gardens

You will find even more birds where there are trees, such as on wasteground and in parks. The birds here are bolder than birds in the country as they are used to being fed by human beings. This means that you can often get much closer to them than you would be able to in the country, and can study their habits more easily. Some of them can become quite tame.

Lakes and ponds in town parks are also very good places to watch birds, especially wildfowl, at close quarters.

Feral pigeons.

13

Garden birds

All the common garden birds originally lived in woodland. They moved to gardens for greater security and a regular food supply. They help gardeners by eating harmful insects and are a delight to birdwatchers. They are shown here drawn more or less to scale.

collared dove

blackbird

song thrush

mistle thrush

house sparrow

blue tit

coal tit

great tit

robin

chaffinch

Collared dove. 31cm. Often seen in parks, gardens and farmyards. Likes to nest in tall trees.

Blackbird. 25cm. The male is jet black with yellow beak and eye-rims. The female is dark brown with brown beak.

Mistle thrush. 27cm. Larger and greyer than the song thrush, with bigger, more spread-out spots.

Song thrush. 23cm. Smaller and browner than the mistle thrush. Smashes snail shells on stones. Song phrases often repeated.

Chaffinch. 15cm. One of our most common birds. Look for it in fields and woods, parks and gardens. Call is a loud 'pink'.

Robin. 14cm. Vigorously asserts its territorial rights with much singing and chest puffing. Juveniles are mottled brown.

Blue tit. 11.5cm. Identified by its blue cap. Common in woods, parks and gardens. Enjoys feeding at bird tables. Very acrobatic.

Coal tit. 11.5cm. Woodland bird that sometimes visits gardens. Identified by a white patch on nape of neck.

Great tit. 14cm. Has central black band on yellow breast and smart black and white head. Main song is a loud, repeated 'tea-cher, tea-cher'.

15

Feeding birds in the garden

Feeding birds is fun all the year round. But in winter, when there is a shortage of natural foods, it is especially important. Buy netted bags filled with peanuts, or containers which you can fill yourself. But don't offer peanuts in the breeding season; young birds cannot digest them.

Bird tables

Other birds may prefer to feed off a bird table. Buy special bird food or put out kitchen scraps such as suet, bacon rind, cheese and over-ripe fruit.

Remember to clean the bird table regularly to prevent the birds getting food poisoning.

A great tit and a pair of blue tits enjoying a bag of peanuts.

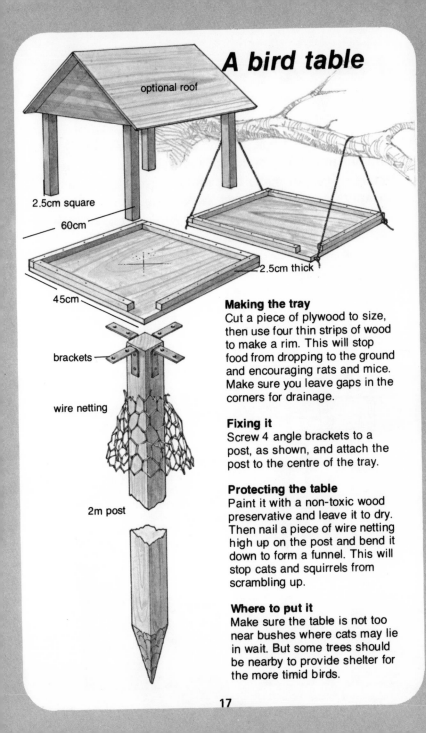

A bird table

optional roof

2.5cm square

60cm

45cm

2.5cm thick

brackets

wire netting

2m post

Making the tray
Cut a piece of plywood to size, then use four thin strips of wood to make a rim. This will stop food from dropping to the ground and encouraging rats and mice. Make sure you leave gaps in the corners for drainage.

Fixing it
Screw 4 angle brackets to a post, as shown, and attach the post to the centre of the tray.

Protecting the table
Paint it with a non-toxic wood preservative and leave it to dry. Then nail a piece of wire netting high up on the post and bend it down to form a funnel. This will stop cats and squirrels from scrambling up.

Where to put it
Make sure the table is not too near bushes where cats may lie in wait. But some trees should be nearby to provide shelter for the more timid birds.

A nesting box

Having a nesting box in your garden is a good way to find out how birds build their nests and care for their young. You can make one yourself quite easily and cheaply. Put it up as early as possible, at least by the beginning of March, so that the birds get used to it. Most birds start to look for nesting sites well in advance.

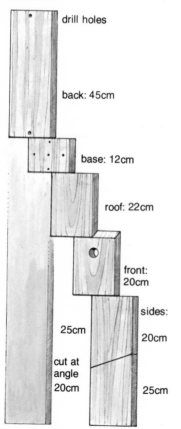

drill holes

back: 45cm

base: 12cm

roof: 22cm

front: 20cm

sides: 20cm

25cm

cut at angle 20cm

25cm

Materials
One rough plank of weather-resistant hardwood, or cedar wood, 16cm wide, 2cm thick and 145cm long; a 16×5cm piece of rubber or leather; copper tacks, two catches and screws for the lid.

Making the box
Cut the wood into lengths as indicated.

Draw a circle on the front section, not less than 12.5cm from the base. This will form the **entrance**. Cut the circle out with an electric drill or make a hole with a hand drill and enlarge it with a chisel.

Drill small **drainage holes** in the base for sanitation.

hole for entrance

FRONT

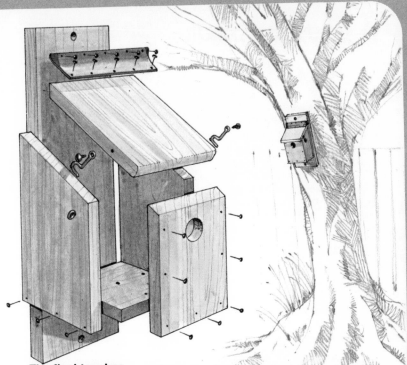

The final touches

Fix the front in position and tack a rubber hinge to the roof section. Then place the roof in position and tack the hinge to the back. Coat the box with a non-toxic wood preservative.

If you want larger birds to nest, you could make an **open-fronted nesting box.** Cut the front section in half to make a larger entrance.

Choosing a site

Choose a site which is sheltered from the midday sun and strong winds – like a tree or building facing east or north-east. Birds like a clear flight path to their nest so place the box away from thick foliage – and out of reach of cats.

Fixing the box

Screw the nesting box firmly in place. It should be tilted slightly downwards to keep out the rain. A perch, to help the birds get into the box, is not necessary and would only help cats and squirrels who want to get at the nestlings.

Caring for the birds

When the baby birds arrive, don't look in on them too often. Once every three days is enough, and then only when the parent birds are away from the nest searching for food. Be just as careful when the youngsters are nearly fledged; you could easily frighten them into leaving the nest too soon.

A bath for birds

The need for water

Birds need water for drinking and bathing in all the year round, especially in built-up areas without ponds or streams. After bathing, birds spread oil from a special gland all over their feathers. This is called 'preening' and keeps their plumage in good condition.

A simple birdbath

You can make a simple birdbath from an old dustbin lid or a large shallow dish. Sink the birdbath into the soil or support it on a couple of bricks. Pile a few stones in the centre as a perching place.

In winter

Birdbaths are very important in winter when the birds' natural supplies of water are frozen over. Fill the bath at least once a day with fresh clean water.

If the bath is raised you can put a night-light underneath to prevent the water freezing. Put the candle under a small flowerpot, or in a perforated tin, to protect it from draughts.

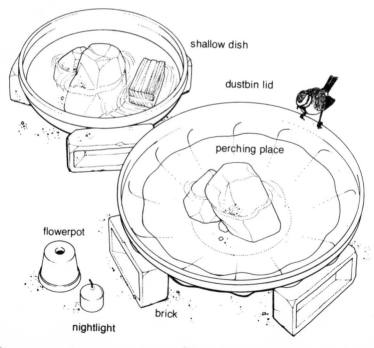

shallow dish

dustbin lid

perching place

flowerpot

brick

nightlight

An ornamental pool

water lilies

perching twig

plastic

45cm deep

75cm deep

polythene sheet

newspaper lining

An ornamental pool can be great fun to build. And it helps to attract birds into the garden.

Building the pool
Ideally it should be on three levels. The **first level** should be at least 75cm deep, for fish to retreat to in very cold or hot weather. You can also grow water lilies there.

The **second level** should be about 45cm deep. Grow oxygenating plants here, such as Canadian pondweed and water milfoil. They will keep the water pure and clean.

The **third level** should be a gently-sloping shallow area at the side, where birds can stand and drink.

Finishing touches
Put a 15cm layer of concrete over the pond bed, or line it with newspapers and spread a layer of heavy-duty polythene over them. Finally put 5–10cm of soil over the bottom.

Attractive marginal plants, such as water mint and yellow flag, can be planted on these shallower shelves or put in pots just below the water-level.

Observing bird behaviour

▲ The elaborate courting ritual of the great crested grebes includes these dance-like movements.

▶ Cormorants have to hold their wings out to dry in the sun as their feathers are not waterproof.

Bird behaviour covers a wide range of fascinating activities, which are well worth studying. All of them are concerned with survival.

Bird language
Birds have had to develop a kind of language to communicate with each other. This includes not only calls and song, but also special movements of the wings, head and tail. They may also flaunt special features, such as a crest or ruff, or a brilliant colour.

A blackbird sunbathing.

Sociable or solitary?

Different species behave very differently, especially when competing for food, perches and nest sites, and in courtship. Some birds are sociable, and feed in flocks. There is safety in numbers. On the other hand, many birds of prey lead an almost solitary life. However, all birds come together in pairs to breed.

Watch different species as they carry out the same activities and note down the differences. How do they feed? How do they defend their territory?

Field trips

Looking further afield

When you have become familiar with the birds you can see near your home, you will probably want to explore further afield. It is a good idea to choose one area, not too far away, and to visit it often. Birds are usually at their most active in the early morning and late-afternoon, so these are the best times to go birdwatching.

Note changes in the bird population; when the first migrants arrive, and when they leave. Make a list of all the birds you recognize. Consult a field guide for the name of any bird you don't know.

Remember that the plumage of some birds changes in the winter. Young birds, too, are often very different from adult birds in colour and markings, and females often differ from males.

A birdwatching map

On a large-scale map of your area, mark in different colours where you have heard birds singing and calling. Birds in flight can be indicated by arrows.

Look out for birds performing threat displays to others of their species. Robins in particular are very aggressive when defending their territory. You may even be able to work out the territorial boundaries on your map. Make notes on the various plants growing nearby. What insect life is there? What are the birds feeding on?

Learning from the experts

Although a great deal can be learned from books, it is much easier to learn from an experienced birdwatcher. If you don't know any birdwatchers, join a birdwatching society or natural history club (*see page 58*).

How to approach birds

The wrong approach
You see a small bird perching on a hedge some
distance away. You want to be able to identify it. You
walk slowly towards it, watching it all the time. But
the bird keeps flying off to perch further along the
hedge. What was your mistake?

The right approach
The bird could see you and knew that you could see
it. And your slow, steady walk and constant gaze
showed that you were interested in it. It will only stay
if you pretend *not* to be interested. Stroll along and
casually turn your back now and then. You can watch
the bird out of the corner of your eye. Eventually you
may get within a few yards, though seldom any
closer.

The wren is a very shy bird. But if
you are patient you may see it in
the undergrowth searching for
insects.

26

The need for patience

You may come across a bird which slips away to hide in the bushes and stays there as long as it thinks you are about. What should you do? Hide! You may have to wait very quietly for a long time. If you are with a friend get him to walk away dangling his coat or jacket from his outstretched hand. The bird may mistake the coat for you and come out of hiding.

If you have binoculars, keep them slung round your neck ready for use. Raise and lower them gently and never make sudden or rapid movements that would alarm the birds. Even if you cannot get close enough to see a bird's coloration and markings, you may still be able to identify it from its silhouette.

Creeping up on a robin.

Can you name these birds?

If you learn to recognize a bird by its silhouette, you will find it much easier to identify the birds you see – especially when they are in flight. How many of these birds do you know? Turn the page upside down to find out the answers.

1. wagtail	11. kestrel
2. thrush or blackbird	12. curlew
3. crow	13. buzzard
4. lapwing	14. owl
5. great crested grebe	15. heron
6. wren	16. swift
7. skylark	17. swallow
8. mallard	18. rook
9. moorhen	19. house martin
10. cuckoo	20. sparrowhawk

28

29

Keeping notes

A useful aid

Most birdwatchers keep notes. After a day's field trip
it is difficult to remember everything in detail. At
regular intervals, stop watching birds and jot down
what you have seen. When you get home, transfer
your notes to a diary – either for your own
satisfaction, or to make a report to a bird club.

Note-taking and simple sketches are useful for
identifying a bird you have never seen before. If you
are lucky enough to see a very rare bird, or a species
in an unusual place, you will need a detailed and
accurate description of your sighting. Later on,
compare your notes with those in the field guide.

A birdwatching notebook.

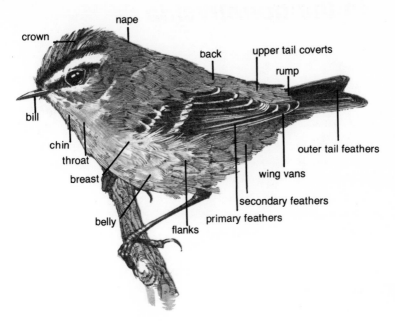

labels: crown, nape, back, upper tail coverts, rump, bill, chin, throat, breast, belly, flanks, primary feathers, secondary feathers, wing vans, outer tail feathers

The parts of a bird

For a proper description it is essential to know what to call the different parts of a bird. If you look at the diagram above, you will see that the terms are not difficult. You will soon get used to them. Write down as many details as possible when you are looking at the bird. Your notes should include the following:

Essential information

1. Date, time and place
2. Type of habitat
3. What the bird is doing
4. The bird's size compared with a bird you know
5. General colour of the plumage
6. The position of unusual colour patches
7. Size, shape and colour of bill, legs and tail
8. Description of call notes or song
9. Movement of wings
10. Whether the bird walked or hopped on the ground

In the countryside

A green woodpecker.

Plenty of variety
The countryside provides many different habitats for
birds to feed and nest in. Few birds nest on the
ground, but watch out for lapwing, yellow wagtail
and skylark nests when you are out walking.
Hedgerow birds include many of those you will see in
parks and gardens as well as some shyer species like
the yellowhammer.

In the woods
Deciduous trees (those which lose their leaves in
winter) often provide holes where birds can nest. In
open woodland you may hear the laughing call of the
green woodpecker. It climbs trees, stripping off the
bark to eat the insects underneath. Another
tree-climbing bird is the nuthatch. It lives on nuts
and tiny insects.

Other woodland birds

In woodland you may well hear the chiff-chaff and the wood warbler singing in the tree tops. They nest in the undergrowth. Two birds of prey to look out for are the tawny owl and the sparrowhawk.

In the open field

The magpie is a woodland bird but can often be seen searching for food in fields nearby. You might see parties of rooks feeding there too, and perhaps even a pheasant. In late summer, wood pigeons move from the woods to the cornfields, often doing a lot of damage to crops. During the cold winter months you will also see large flocks of jackdaws, starlings, thrushes and finches searching for food in the fields.

Pheasants looking for food.

Birds of the countryside

The countryside is rich in bird life. Look for birds in the hedgerows, on arable and pasture land, perching on telegraph poles or in different kinds of woodland: deciduous, coniferous (or pine), and mixed.

Chiffchaff. 11cm. Song is a continuous 'chiff-chaff, chiff-chaff'. Looks almost identical to the willow warbler.

Wood pigeon. 40cm. Europe's largest dove. Look for it on farmland and in woods, parks and gardens.

Yellowhammer. 16.5cm. Found in country lanes and farmyards. Song is a high-pitched chi-chi-chi-chi-chi-chweee.

Tawny owl. 38cm. Hunts by night. Hoots, and calls 'kee-wick'. Roosts during day.

Goldfinch. 12cm. Familiar sight in late summer and autumn feeding on thistle heads.

chiffchaff

wood pigeon

tawny owl

yellowhammer

Great spotted woodpecker.
23cm. Call is repeated loud,
sharp 'kik'. In spring drums on
dead wood with bill.

great spotted
woodpecker

Linnet. 13cm. Common in open
country where there are hedges
and bushes. Male has red crown
and breast in summer.

Nuthatch. 14cm. An agile
tree-climber. It will wedge a nut
in tree-bark crevice and hammer
it open with its bill.

nuthatch

Skylark. 18cm. Nests on ground
in open country. Sings while
hovering so high in the sky it is
often beyond sight.

Magpie. 45cm (including a 25cm
tail). Notorious for hoarding
glittering objects. Identified by
pied plumage and long tail.

magpie

skylark

linnet

goldfinch

On inland waters

Some of our most attractive birds are found either on or near fresh water. With luck, you may even spot the brightly coloured kingfisher flashing down to catch a fish.

Ducks

The smallest European duck is the teal. Like the mallard it is a dabbler; it takes food from on, or just below, the surface of the water. The tufted duck and pochard are diving ducks; they go right under the water to feed on plants, snails and other water creatures. When danger threatens, dabbling ducks spring almost vertically from the water.

Feeding the ducks.

▲ The sapphire flash of a kingfisher.

On larger stretches of water – rivers, lakes and reservoirs – grebes are common. The largest is the great crested grebe, easily distinguished during the breeding season by its double horned crest.

At the water's edge

You may be lucky enough to see a heron standing immobile, ready to strike at a small fish or frog. Other waterside birds include the reed warbler, with its melodious song, the sedge warbler and the reed bunting.

On marshes and damp grassland you may see wading birds – curlews, golden plover or snipe – or even a yellow wagtail. The favourite haunt of the white-chested dipper is a fast-running stream in a hilly district. Watch it diving, swimming and making little curtsies from its perch in midstream.

Birds of the waterside

Birds are attracted to inland waters where they can
feed well and find safe nesting places. Some species
are threatened by the reclamation of marshes. Many
others have been saved by pollution control – often
because it has protected the fish they feed on.

tufted duck

heron

Canada
goose

dipper

teal

Canada goose. 96cm. North American species introduced in many parks. Now it is often found breeding in the wild.

Grey heron. 90cm. Common where there is open water or marshland. Nests in colonies, usually in trees.

Reed warbler. 13cm. Summer visitor. Look for it in reed beds. Song helps to distinguish it from other waterside warblers.

Tufted duck. 43cm. Diving duck. Widely distributed. The black and white drake is easily recognized; the female is brown.

Teal. 35cm. Smallest European duck. Surface-feeding. Both sexes have green speculum. Often breeds near rushy pools.

Reed bunting. 15cm. Male has conspicuous black head and white collar in spring. Rather sparrow-like at other times.

Coot. 38cm. All-black body with white facial shield. Common on open water where it frequently dives for food.

Moorhen. 33cm. Common by ponds, lakes and rivers. Swims with jerky head movements. Note white patches under tail, and red facial shield.

Dipper. 18cm. Confined to fast-flowing streams on high ground. Like a large wren in shape. Swims on and under water.

reed bunting

reed warbler

great crested grebe

moorhen

coot

By the sea

Seashores can be rocky, sandy or muddy. Sometimes they are backed by cliffs, or there may be shingle, sand dunes or an estuary. Each type of coast has its own variety of birds.

Estuaries and mud flats

Muddy shores and estuaries are marvellous for birdwatching, especially in winter. They are open, comparatively safe feeding grounds. Here you may see several types of wader: curlew, oyster-catcher, redshank, ringed plover, knot and dunlin. The handsome shelduck is common, too.

If you ever make a sea trip, be sure to look out for birds of the open sea like the Manx shearwater and the storm petrel. These birds rarely come ashore except to breed.

Oyster-catchers on mud flats.

A colony of puffins.

Cliffs and rock faces
Steep cliffs and rocky islands are the favourite
breeding places of many seabirds, some of which
come together in their thousands to form colonies.

Gulls
Although they are usually associated with the sea,
gulls can often be found inland. The black-headed
gull, for example, is common in cities.

Immature gulls can be difficult to identify. Mostly
brown at first, they only gradually acquire the adult
plumage. Terns look rather like gulls, but have
forked tails and black caps.

Birds of the seashore

Many different species of birds are to be found in coastal areas. Birds on sandy or shingly shores depend on the tide to wash up food. Others catch fish from the sea and may only come ashore to nest.

Redshank. 28cm. Often ahead of other species in calling alarm: a loud 'tew-hee-hee'. Breeds on moorland and saltmarsh.

Common gull. 41cm. Mainly nests inland and on moors and marshes; sometimes also on islands and shingle beaches. Note yellow legs.

Gannet. 90cm. Expert diver; sometimes drops from heights of more than 40 metres. Breeds in vast colonies.

Cormorant. 90cm. A big, dark bird with white patches on thighs in summer. Easily confused with the smaller shag.

Common tern. 35cm. Nests in colonies on beaches, rocky islands and saltmarshes. All terns are graceful in flight.

Black-headed gull. 38cm. Very common on coasts and also far inland – even in cities. Has chocolate-brown head in summer.

Lesser black-backed gull. 53cm. Very similar to the herring gull in size and appearance, but with a darker grey back.

Shelduck. 65cm. Common on mud-flats and estuaries. Drake and duck look alike. Feeds chiefly on small shore creatures.

Herring gull. 56cm. Abundant around coasts; frequent visitor inland. Very adaptable in its diet; largely a scavenger.

redshank

common gull

cormorant

lesser black-backed gull

gannet

black-headed gull

common tern

shelduck

herring gull

knot

43

In remote regions

On the moors

Moorland soil is peaty, acidic, and often very wet. The wetter moors are the haunt of several species of wader. Common moorland sounds are the bubbling song and melancholy call of the curlew. This bird moves to the coast in winter.

Drier moors are covered with heather and frequented by the grouse and the golden plover. You will also find the meadow pipit and the skylark here. They feed almost exclusively on insects. In gorse and bracken you may see the whinchat. All these birds nest on the ground. So do some moorland birds of prey, such as the short-eared owl, the merlin and the hen-harrier.

The curlew tries to attract attention away from its nest by trailing its wings on the ground.

A golden eagle amid the craggy rocks.

In the mountains

High in the mountains there is little to attract birds. Vegetation is sparse and temperatures often very low. A bird has to be hardy to survive. The snow bunting, ptarmigan and dotterel are all found on high mountain slopes.

Mountain crags are also the nesting sites of birds of prey, such as the golden eagle, the buzzard and the peregrine falcon. The largest member of the crow family, the raven, nests on moorland ledges. Listen for its deep honking calls as it hunts in pairs or small groups for carrion.

Dippers and grey wagtails may be seen by fast-flowing mountain streams. In rocky country, where there are scattered bushes and trees, look out also for the ring ouzel. It looks like a blackbird but has a white crescent on its breast.

Birds of moorland and mountain

Mountain slopes provide shelter for fierce birds of prey, which feed on small birds and mammals, as well as for the hardy ptarmigan and grouse. Other moorland birds like the ring ouzel and the curlew move south for the winter.

raven

ring ouzel

Ring ouzel. 24 cm. Similar to blackbird; has white crescent across breast. Inhabits rocky country with scattered trees.

Raven. 74 cm. Common only in wild mountainous areas. Mainly feeds on small animals and carrion.

Kestrel. 34 cm. Common bird of prey, also found on farmland and in cities. Hovers while searching for its prey of small mammals.

Wheatear. 14.5 cm. Found on barren, rocky hillsides and open country. Among the first migrants to arrive in spring.

Golden eagle. 75–88 cm. Europe's most common eagle. Habitat mainly mountain tops. Usually nests on rocky ledge.

Lapwing. 30 cm. A bird of field, moor and marshland. Eats insects, including many harmful pests. Calls 'pee-wit'.

lapwing

buzzard

kestrel

wheatear

short-eared owl

meadow pipit

Short-eared owl. 38cm. Look for it on moorland and in open country.

golden plover

Golden plover. 28cm. Nests on moorland. Has black and gold speckled upper parts.

Whinchat. 13cm. Summer visitor. Nests in rough vegetation.

Meadow pipit. 14.5cm. Nests on the ground in rough open country.

whinchat

47

Only visiting: migration

A swallow building its nest under an overhanging roof.

Birds that stay where they are all the year round are known as residents. Other species that look for warmer weather in winter are called migrants. Some migrants, like the swallow, may travel very long distances. Others, like many waders, travel shorter distances to winter on the coasts.

Passage migrants

These are birds that pass through Europe in late spring and autumn on their way to and from their breeding grounds. They are particularly interesting to birdwatchers as they can only be spotted during a few weeks in the year.

White-fronted geese flying south in formation.

Keeping track of migration patterns

Migratory movements are studied in several ways: by direct observation at special bird observatories, or by bird-ringing schemes. Thousands of birds are trapped and ringed every year. The recovered rings show where the birds go and what routes they take. High-powered radar equipment has also been useful in tracking migrant birds. No one knows exactly how birds navigate, but possibly they use the sun and stars to find their way.

Other sorts of movement occur besides migration. Some species, such as the crossbill and the waxwing, make spectacular *irruptions* from one area into another. This apparently happens when the bird population becomes too large for the available food supply. There are also birds which move seasonally, but randomly, in all directions. This is called *dispersal*.

Some migrant birds

In spring, summer and early autumn, there is plenty of food for birds. But when the weather turns colder and food becomes scarce, many birds leave their breeding grounds and fly to warmer lands.

blackcap

nightingale

female

fieldfare

redstart

redwing

yellow wagtail

sand martin

swift

house martin

cuckoo

Blackcap. 14cm. A member of the warbler family. Like most warblers it eats insects, and migrates mainly by night.

Redstart. 14cm. Summer visitor. Found in parks and gardens.

Redwing. 21cm. In summer lives in Scandinavia, Iceland and Russia. Winters in warmer parts of Europe.

Nightingale. 16.5cm. Arrives from Africa in late spring. Beautiful song.

Fieldfare. 25.5cm. In winter found in large flocks feeding in open country.

Swallow. 19cm. Migrates from Africa. Often returns to the same nest year after year.

House martin. 13cm. Easily recognized by white rump. Tail less forked than swallow's.

Sandmartin. 12cm. Has a brown breast band. Nests in colonies in cliffs or sandy banks.

Swift. 16.5cm. Feeds on insects caught on the wing. It is not related to the swallow.

Cuckoo. 33cm. Lays its eggs in another bird's nest. Only the male sings 'cuckoo'. Migrates to tropical Africa.

Listening to birds

A wren: a small bird with a loud voice.

With practice, you can distinguish different species of birds by their voices. Some birds, like the chiff-chaff, have a song made up of only two or three notes. Others sing complex tunes.

The meaning of birdsong

Birds usually sing to proclaim their ownership of territory or to attract a mate. Other sounds have special meanings. 'Call' notes are those which birds use to let others know their species, sex and what they are doing. Birds feeding together in flocks or migrating together by night, keep in touch with 'contact' notes. Then there is the more obvious 'alarm' note, like the raucous burst of sound a blackbird makes. Mild anxiety is expressed as a quiet 'cluck'.

Recording birdsong

Equipment

Use a lightweight, battery-powered **cassette recorder** for everyday use, and for taking on field trips. Higher quality recordings can be made on a **reel-to-reel recorder.**

The **microphone** is important. Use a moving coil, or cardioid, microphone with an extension lead. Remember, it is dangerous to use a mains recorder outside in damp conditions.

Simple recordings.

Interesting recordings can be made even from a window ledge. Study the mimicry of starlings, or the language of sparrows or great tits. You could even try to analyse the dawn chorus.

Using a reflector

To record sound over a greater distance, make a **parabolic reflector** using the bowl of an old electric fire. Face the microphone into the bowl, and stretch an old nylon stocking over the bowl to reduce wind noise.

Try comparing the dialects of chaffinches from different areas, or play a recording of a bird back to it and observe its reaction. You can gradually build up a library of bird songs.

parabolic reflector

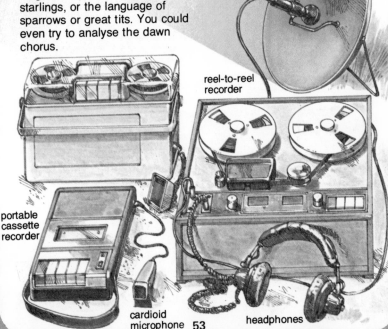

reel-to-reel recorder

portable cassette recorder

cardioid microphone 53

headphones

How to photograph birds

The camera
A simple camera is good enough for photographing birds for your notebook or diary. But if you want to take really good photographs, you will need a single-lens reflex camera where focusing is 'through the lens'. As the lenses are interchangeable, this camera can be used for both close-ups and long-range photography.

But an expensive camera does not guarantee good photographs. A lot depends on how you compose the picture, and on pressing the shutter at exactly the right moment. Don't worry if your first efforts are disappointing.

▲ A typical 'hide'.

Using a hide
Your biggest problem will be getting close enough to the birds you want to photograph. One way is to use a 'hide'.

A hide is a box-like frame covered with canvas, in which you can conceal yourself from the birds you want to study. Mesh-covered slits enable you to look out without being seen. The camera, on a tripod, is concealed in the hide, and the lens projects through a sleeve-like pocket.

If you are good with your hands, you could make one. Let the birds get used to the hide for several days before you use it. Make sure, too, that it is in a good position.

▲ Stalking a bird through bushes.

The film
Birds move fast: to 'freeze' them in mid-flight you must use a fast shutter speed and a fast film. A slow colour film will give you pictures with a clearer image, but any movement will show as a blur. Try experimenting with different films.

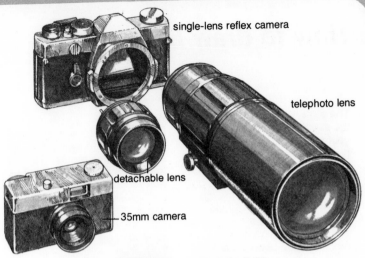

single-lens reflex camera

telephoto lens

detachable lens

35mm camera

▲ A photograph taken with ordinary lens. It is difficult to get really close to the subject.

▼ The same photograph, taken from the same place, but this time with a telephoto lens. The telephoto lens makes it possible to get in much closer to the subject. But it also means that you have to be more precise in focusing the camera.

Telephoto lens

A more expensive method of obtaining close-up pictures is by using a telephoto lens. These more powerful lenses have less 'depth of field' over long distances. This means your focusing has to be spot-on.

▲ A more unusual subject: starlings anting.

Choice of subject

Why not photograph unusual activities like starlings 'anting' (see above). The garden is a good place to start. Take pictures of groups of birds feeding at the bird table.

How to draw birds

The more you know about birds, the easier it is to picture them in your mind – so when drawing birds, choose the ones you know best.

Drawing tools
You will need a pencil (use a fairly soft one like a 2B), a small pad of cartridge paper and a soft rubber. Some people use a chisel-shaped pencil as it can make either fine or thick strokes.

Be relaxed
Don't tense your arm muscles when you are drawing: use an easy, rhythmic motion. Try not to dig into the paper. And don't worry if at first your outline is not very good – rough it in very lightly, then pick out the lines that look right and go over them more strongly. Rub out the rest. With practice you may get the correct lines straightaway.

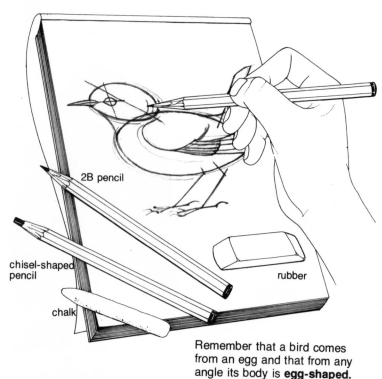

2B pencil

chisel-shaped
pencil

rubber

chalk

Remember that a bird comes from an egg and that from any angle its body is **egg-shaped.**

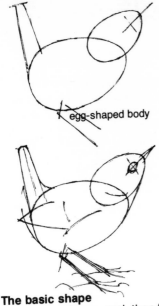

egg-shaped body

The basic shape
Start by drawing an oval, then fill in the head, wings, feet and legs. Make them look as though they grow from the body, and are not just stuck on.

The feet should look firmly planted on the ground or perch. Don't attempt to draw in every detail of its plumage and markings, but aim for a general impression.

Giving it character
Instead of making a black blob for the bird's eye, show a little reflected light in the pupil – your bird will look much more alive.

Make lots of quick sketches of moving birds for practice. Draw in only the essential lines.

Notice the features which distinguish one type of bird from another: what makes an owl 'owlish', or a duck 'duckish'. Emphasize these in your drawing, even to the point of caricature. At least nobody will mistake what you're drawing!

Learning from drawing
By trying to draw a bird, you look at it more closely. So even if the end result isn't wonderful, the effort won't have been wasted.

▲ Pick out special features

Reference section

Organizations

Joining a club or society is the best way to learn more about birdwatching. You can write to:

American Birding
  Association
P.O. Box 4335
Austin, Texas 78765
Publication: *Birding*

American Ornithologists
  Union, Inc.
National Museum of Natural
  History
Smithsonian Institution
Washington, DC 20560
Publications: *The Auk,
  Ornithological Monographs*

Bird Friends Society
Essex, Connecticut 06426
Publication: *Wild Bird Guide*

Bird Populations Institute
Kansas State University
P.O. Box 637
Manhattan, Kansas 66502
Publication: *The Bird Watch*

Brooks Bird Club
707 Warwood Avenue
Wheeling, West Virginia
  26003
Publications: *The Redstart,
The Mailbag*

Cooper Ornithological
  Society
% Stephen M. Russell
Department of Ecology and
  Evolutionary Biology
University of Arizona
Tucson, Arizona 85721
Publication: *The Condor,
  Pacific Coast Avifauna*

Cornell University
  Laboratory of Ornithology
159 Sapsucker Woods Road
Ithaca, New York 14850
Publications: *The Living
  Bird, Members' Newsletter*

Hawk Mountain Sanctuary
  Association
R.D. 2
Kempton, Pennsylvania
  19529
Publication: *Members'
  Newsletter*

Massachusetts Audubon
  Society, Inc.
South Great Road
Lincoln, Massachusetts
  01773
Publications: *Newsletter,
  Man and Nature*
  (yearbook), *Curious
  Naturalist*

National Audubon Society
950 Third Avenue
New York, New York 10022
Publications: *Audubon,
  Audubon Leader, American
  Birds*

National Wildlife Federation
1412 Sixteenth Street, NW
Washington, D.C. 20036
Publications: *National*
Wildlife, International
Wildlife, Ranger Rick's
Nature Magazine

Wilson Ornithological
  Society
%Jerome A. Jackson
Department of Zoology
Mississippi State University
Mississippi State, MS 39762
Publication: *The Wilson*
Bulletin

Bird reserves

What better way to see
America than to search out
the lands which are undeve-
loped and carefully set aside
for wildlife, especially birds.
Birdwatchers can walk
through the most beautiful
areas in this country. They
can breathe some of the
cleanest air on earth.

A major reason for the
growing popularity of
birdwatching is the beauty
and interest found in the
birds themselves. It can be
fun and absorbing not only to
recognize a bird but also to
learn about it and notice
where it is, what it is doing,
and, if possible, why.

The National Parks and
National Wildlife Refuges
provide resting and breeding
places for birds and other
wildlife. Extensive notes on
various types of wildlife are
kept by these institutions.

Recently an increasing
number of arboretums, public
gardens, environmental edu-
cation centers, and other
places with moderately large
tracts of land and water to
preserve are discovering,
cherishing, and listing the
birds that fly in. Bird sanctuaries vary as to their nature.
Rugged areas, good picnic
grounds, or even city parks,
may be bird refuges.

On February 18, 1929,
Congress enacted the Migratory Bird Conservation Act
which authorized the Federal
Government to acquire land
and water areas for waterfowl
refuges. The legislation set up
a Migratory Bird Conservation Commission to study and
approve the purchase or lease
of such areas as sanctuaries
for ducks, geese, and other
migratory birds.

Since then, the commis-
sion has overseen the estab-
lishment of 311 refuges in 42
states — over 10 million
acres of marshes, prairie pot-
holes, hardwood bottoms,
and other havens for waterfowl, scattered from Maine to
California and from Washington to Florida. These refuges

are strategically located along the four major north-south waterfowl migration routes to provide breeding habitats, sheltered resting places, and safe wintering areas for the birds.

For information about wildlife refuges in your area contact the *U.S. Fish and Wildlife Service; Migratory Bird Conservation Commission; Washington, DC 20240.*

Nature trails

A nature trail is a sign-posted route through an area of natural interest. Points of interest (either animals, plants, trees or birds) are explained by means of panels at appropriate places, or by numbered posts or boards and a printed trail guide.

Many nature trails are of interest to birdwatchers, but there are too many to list all of them here. All state parks have nature trails. The following are just a few of the many:

Acadia National Park,
Bar Harbor, Maine 04609

Cape Cod National Seashore
South Wellfleet,
Massachusetts 02663

Cape Hatteras National
  Seashore
P.O. Box 675,
Manteo, North Carolina
  27954

Great Swamp National
  Wildlife Refuge
R.D. 1, Box 148
Basking Ridge, New Jersey
  07920

Everglades National Park
P.O. Box 279
Homestead, Florida 33030

Montezuma National
  Wildlife Refuge
R.D. #1 Box 232
Seneca Falls, New York
  13148

Yellowstone National Park
P.O. Box 168
Yellowstone National Park,
  Wyoming 82190

Monahans Sandhills State
  Park
Box 1738
Monahans, Texas 79756

Bird checklists

Bird checklists are everchanging indexes to the contents of bird refuges. Checklists are, at their best, almost an art form. Illustrations and graphics are striking and clearly printed to be read outdoors in fog, frost, or bright sunlight. Very good lists are at once practical and attractive, printed on narrow widths in pocket-sized flip-page style with pages of graduated length, with each page labeled at the base so that all labels show. Helpful information and small drawings of birds may be included.

Many refuges supply these checklists to visitors.

Books and field guides

Audubon Society Field Guide to North American Birds: Eastern Region by J. Bull and J. Ferrand Jr. Western Region by M. Udvardy (Alfred A. Knopf, 1977)

Backyard Bird Watcher by George H. Harrison (Simon and Schuster, 1979)

Birds of North America by Chandler S. Robbins, et al. (Golden Press, 1966)

Birdwatcher's Bible by George Laycock (Doubleday and Co., Inc., 1976)

Birdwatcher's Guide to Wildlife Sanctuaries by Jessie Kitching (Arco Publishing Company, 1975)

A Field Guide to Birds Nests in the Eastern U.S. by Hal H. Harrison (Houghton Mifflin, 1975)

A Field Guide to Birds Nests in the Western U.S. by Hal H. Harrison (Houghton Mifflin, 1979)

Fifty Birds of Town and City by Robert Hines (U.S. Government Printing Office)

A Guide to Birdwatching by Joseph J. Hickey (Dover Publications, 1975)

Guide to National Wildlife Refuges by Laura and William Riley (Doubleday and Co., Inc., 1979)

Guide to North American Bird Clubs by Jon E. Rickert (Avian Publications, 1978)

Illustrated Handbook of North American Birds by E.M. Reilly Jr. (McGraw-Hill, 1968)

More Wildlife on Your Property by Harry L. Gillam (Virginia Commission of Game and Inland Fisheries, 1973)

Random House Book of Birds by E.S. Austin and O.L. Austin Jr. (Random House, 1970)

World of Birds by James Fisher and Roger Tory Peterson (Crescent Books, 1977)

Glossary

Anting When a bird allows ants to stream over its body or applies them directly to its plumage. (Ants squirt out formic acid which probably kills off the bird's parasites.)

Colony Large group of breeding birds.

Crest A tuft of feathers rising from a bird's crown.

Habitat The particular kind of environment inhabited by a bird, animal or plant, e.g. the seashore.

Hood Distinctive coloured plumage covering most of the head.

Immature A bird after it has left the nest but before it is able to breed.

Incubation Keeping eggs warm to hatch them.

Irruption Sudden mass movement of birds beyond the areas they normally live in.

Migration The mass movement of some birds in different seasons from one locality to another.

Mobbing An attack on an enemy by a group of birds.

Peck order The order in which different species of birds dominate one another. (A bird that is higher in the peck order than another will feed first.)

Raptor A bird of prey (excluding owls).

Scavenger Bird or animal that eats scraps of food and dead animals.

Species Group of animals, birds or plants able to breed with each other. (The common names of familiar birds usually denote their species, e.g. robin, songthrush.)

Summer visitor A bird that breeds in this country but migrates in winter.

Territory An area defended by a bird against intruders of the same species.

Wildfowl The family of ducks, geese and swans.

Winter visitor A bird only present in this country outside the breeding season.

Index

The numbers in **bold** refer to illustrations.

ALONE UNTIL TOMORROW

ALONE

UNTIL TOMORROW

BY LILIANE GIUDICE

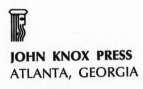

JOHN KNOX PRESS
ATLANTA, GEORGIA

This book is a translation of *Ohne meinen Mann: Aufzeichnungen einer Witwe,* published by Kreuz-Verlag, Stuttgart, Germany. © Kreuz-Verlag Stuttgart 1970.

Library of Congress Cataloging in Publication Data

Guidice, Liliane.
    Alone until tomorrow.

    Translation of Ohne meinen Mann.
    1. Bereavement—Personal narratives. I. Title.
BF575.G7G8413   242′.4   73-16912
ISBN 0-8042-1982-6

CONTENTS

How many widows are standing at this very moment on a train platform somewhere with no one waiting for them; how many are hoping at this very moment to hear the telephone ring, if only for a few seconds to hear a voice in the empty house; how many are rushing at this very moment through the city in order to hide their loneliness, and have no one to hurry home to? In a million places throughout the world at this very moment, there beats the heart of a woman who has lost her husband.

For these women and for myself I wanted to write this little book, whether anyone ever reads it or not. Perhaps it may comfort at least one widow. To learn that someone else suffers like oneself may be a comfort, simply because one feels understood, if only by a stranger. All women who loved their husbands suffer the same anguish. But all anguish changes, and the way it changes is what distinguishes those who mourn.

The wonderful alchemy of suffering: it strikes me as a miracle how a torment that threatens to annihilate one, which one at first passionately resists, can become a source of strength. I would like to write about this miracle. Every woman who mourns can experience it, even if at first she does not believe in it, and after long struggle each can be raised from her suffering to joyous confidence. When? During mourning one must learn to wait. We must not be less patient than God.

THE CHARMED CIRCLE

Something So Strange

"Death is something so strange that, notwithstanding all experience, one does not consider it possible in the case of an object of our affection; it always takes place as something unbelievable and unexpected. It is, so to speak, an impossibility that suddenly becomes reality" (Goethe).

The doctor came thorugh the door that Oki had just gone through and said, "He is dead." Heart attack. An impossibility had suddenly become reality. Today, years later, I still have not found any words that can express the beginning of the path of suffering more accurately. Every woman, believer or unbeliever, prepared for the death of her husband or taken by surprise, resists by taking refuge behind the wall of impossibility.

I was fifty-three years old, and despite war and air raids, I had never seen a dead man. Apart from the Bible I had no knowledge of death, which we increasingly exclude from our daily lives instead of including it, not with dread and loathing, but with confidence and in the hope that it will bring us into a realm of joy.

The doctor was waiting. I had to say something I shrank from saying: "I want to see my husband." Were Oki's eyes open? I thought one shut the eyes of the dead, but I did not know when. I was afraid of meeting a fixed stare. I was relieved; Oki had his eyes shut, his expression was peaceful, only very serious. Before, it had been smiles and happiness, even in difficult times. I sat down beside him. Was his hand cold? I touched it hesitantly, and it was warm.

I began to speak softly to him. They say that for the first three days the dead can hear the words we whisper to them. I will not smile at this superstition, for it was natural for me to speak with Oki and I hoped unconsciously that he would hear me.

Conversation with a dead man, conversation full of tender devotion, because one would like to give the dead one's love to accompany him on the way — it will be a long absence. A shy conversation, for a mystery has intervened between us. In sleep you also parted from me. May God accompany you. I said God, although he was far distant. You lie beside me and I stroke your hand. I have a sense of peace; I am happy, because I love.

It was a final gift of grace before comprehension dawned.

The Man in Black

Someone came into the room and took me into an adjoining room. A man in black was standing there, speaking with a subdued voice and asking what kind of coffin I would like to have, oak or fir.

Oki had just brought the flower boxes into the garden, singing; then we had gone to the sanatorium to see his doctor, because he was not feeling well; and now I was being asked about his coffin. I screamed at the man and felt unsure of myself. Surely Oki wasn't really dead?

I demanded to see the doctor who had made the mistake. I wanted to have a room for Oki in the sanatorium; that was impossible. I did not know that it is forbidden to die in the sanatorium, and if it nevertheless happens, the dead are removed quickly and unobtrusively so as not to frighten the living. Then I wanted to take Oki home. "I must do whatever you request," said the doctor, "but please leave him in peace." But where were Oki and I to have peace? I didn't know where the dead were taken; I only wanted to be beside him in some room, and continue talking to him.

When I Realized

Suddenly I lost all my strength; I had to go home to friends who would help me fight for Oki. On the way to the car someone ran after me: "You forgot your coat." I stared blankly at the woman;

she laid Oki's coat over my arm. Now with brutal finality the impossible became reality for me. Even when the experience of death is eased by the care of loving people and one does not have to choose a coffin within the hour of a man's death, the brutal strokes remain, and they were only the first of my period of suffering.

"The disappearance of a person from this earth is horrible" (Jeremias Gotthelf). It was horrible. I fled to the car. The coat that Oki had just taken off was lying across my lap. I was breathing its odor, not daring to touch it. We drove past the large homes, past the workmen that Oki had just seen. No, not we; *I* drove past.

Now the pain had begun, and now God was present. It was as though he were trying to tear me to shreds. It was God that horrified me. My God, my God — that was all I could think. When my mind let go of these words I fell into an abyss. A world in which one cannot cling to what one loves most is a world in which one drowns if God is not there. "The dread of thee makes my flesh creep, and I stand in awe of thy decrees." I was in the grip of the same fear as had gripped the psalmist thousands of years before. I could not pray, I could only whimper uncomprehendingly: My God, my God. The word sustained me.

Wheels

I entered our dwelling with Oki's coat over my arm. He would have known what had to be done now; I was alone and had no one to ask. Death means that one is compelled to set wheels in motion; I surmised as much but hesitated. I paced back and forth in the house, pursued by the silence. Then I called the undertaker, and thus a machinery was set in motion at the funeral home. The undertaker came, and the man in black was there once again. I had to decide on the ceremony, send telegrams, make phone calls, now that God had intervened — God, who was holding me by the collar and shaking me. I made all the wrong decisions, but it made no difference what funeral rites were carried out before the time of burial.

The First Night

The first night had to come sometime; sometime I had to take off the dress in which Oki had last seen me. I kept deferring it, as though his gaze were still riveted on me. I lay on the couch and stared at his bed.

He would be lying on this bed now if I had had the strength to fight for his body. Now he was alone in the mortuary chapel. Everything is all right, and I shouldn't worry, said the friends who had come to the sanatorium, where Oki had already been taken away. Tomorrow I will visit him.

If there are any prayers that are only groans, I prayed. The night did not seem long; there is an intensity of grief in which time loses its meaning.

A Visit to the Dead

"The body is so adorned because one cannot adorn the soul, and yet one wishes to send it forth pure and sparkling, since it is rid of its bonds, having withstood a hard and varied battle" (Plutarch).

I went to Oki. Now I know where the dead are brought. One rings the bell as one would ring the bell when paying a call on the living, only here a deep gong sounds. The attendant comes from the far reaches of the cemetery and opens the door to one of the chambers behind the apse. The dead are locked up. The chamber was narrow, lined with white tile, and had a large window that stood open. The first thing I saw was branches dancing in the sunlight, because I hesitated for a long time before I dared look at Oki. He lay in a coffin, wearing a white shroud, his head on a white pillow, his hands folded. The doctor had shut his eyes, a stranger had bathed and dressed him. *I* had done nothing for him.

How had he been brought here? I had not seen his hearse.

Today hearses hurry unobtrusively through the streets as though ashamed of their burden. As a child in Spain, I was quite familiar with the sight of the unwieldy carriages with their black horses and black plumes, drawn at a slow pace through the streets. Everyone stopped reverently as the carriage passed; men removed their hats, women crossed themselves.

Oki's coffin was ugly, and the white shroud upset me, because it looked out of place on him. As a young girl I had read with amazement of a woman who was tortured by fear of dying before she would be able to weave her shroud. The lack of a shroud she felt to be a disgrace. Even the poorest of the poor had to have a shroud and a bridal dress. When that woman was laid out, the entire village would pass by to pay their last earthly respects and see whether she was wearing fine linen — the final tyranny of society, even against the poor. The sister of T., whose husband was called from his honeymoon to the front during the First World War, where he was immediately killed, had wanted to be buried in her bridal dress and veil. As if by a miracle, the features of the old woman are said to have regained the loveliness of her youth underneath the veil. Who today thinks of what he will wear in his coffin?

Here the dead wear white — white, the color of light. "If the color of light is associated with death, the dominant idea is not the destruction of the body, but the passage of the soul into life in the realm of light" (Bachofen). Words for later — the realm of light lies far distant when one is tortured by grief.

The man in black was there; he was always present until the moment of burial, unobtrusive, like a master of ceremonies. Now he took a brush from his pocket and brushed a strand of Oki's hair smooth, for the wind was blowing through the open window. Then he stepped aside, as at a demonstration. Did Oki still belong to me?

At my next visit I brought him a rose, his favorite flower. It was beautiful to the point of mockery — the red flower in those hands, which, after his eyes, I had loved most. The folded hands gradually became paler, narrower; the face grew more serious and took on a carved look. On the third day the peaceful features had become severe; nature was doing her work, quietly and precisely. I asked to have the coffin shut; a son should not see his father so.

I was not present when the coffin was shut; I did not want to know when Oki's body, which I had loved, was taken away from me. Perhaps I would have screamed, "Don't! He'll suffocate!"

I Don't Want to Wake Up

I am not awake yet, but I feel as though something terrible is about to happen. I do not want to wake up! I know when I awake I will be in a hell. I want to sleep, sleep, not suffer! Inexorably comes awakening and the reminder: Oki is no longer there; he's lying in the mortuary chapel. The day after tomorrow he will be buried. I am alone.

Grotesquerie

I was sunk in the abyss of grief, and people expected me to put on mourning. I did not have a black dress because Oki did not like black, and on his last day above the earth I had to wear the color he had refused to see me in. In the past, women wore white in mourning, as the color of light, because the departed was on his way to a new life. The color of light would have made more sense to me than the color of night, but why should I have to bear witness to my grief by any color at all?

The shopping trip with a friend was ghastly. A black dress, a black hat, black shoes, black stockings, black gloves. Only once did I rebel. In the first black dress I tried on I looked dreadful, and I requested something different. Did I love Oki any the less because I did not want to be ugly? I had a bad conscience. It would have been kinder to let me wear bright colors in mourning than to drag me through the stores. What respect did it show toward Oki — for he was the one concerned — for me to stand at his grave in black widow's weeds? All I wanted was to converse with him as long as his body was still above the ground, and not to let anything divert my attention from him.

The mortuary machinery ran its course, in the company of friends. So much commotion about a man lying quietly dead. Why the hurry to advertise the death of one's beloved to the world in an obituary notice? Oki's death only mattered to me, his son, and a few others. How good it would have been to wait until later to ponder on words for his death, his last communication with the living, once his body was committed to the earth. Now I was incapable of finding words and left the task to friends, only asking that they include the phrase "Lord over life and death . . ." For Oki's death was God's affair.

Disguise

On the day of the burial I looked at the mourning laid out for me to wear; all I felt was hostility. I put on the dress. Oki would have said, "You should get something smarter." When he talked about clothes, he liked to use expressions he learned from his mother. When I came to the shoes, of which he claimed I never had enough, he would have said triumphantly, "You see, you still don't have the right shoes, and for my burial at that!" The turban he would have placed on his head, as he did all my hats, then done a dance with it on until we both sank exhausted into a chair. I had to think of such things and act as though he were standing behind me. Otherwise I wouldn't have had the strength to get dressed.

Mechanically I reached for my makeup, then hesitated. No, I was Oki's wife, I was still his wife and would remain so, as he had loved me; I would not become a wretched widow and let myself go to pieces.

The more black I put on, the more I felt encased in armor. When my friend came in, she looked me over critically and asked me to take off the black stockings — only people in the sticks still wore black stockings. I put on another pair. How was I supposed to know whether black stockings were presently in fashion or not?

The Tulips Bloom

When I went out the door to get into the limousine for the ride to the cemetery, I suddenly shrank back. In the garden in front of the house the tulips, which someone who once lived in the house had set out, had opened. They must have been an inferior variety, for only a few wretched, spindly little plants braved the frosts of March, as Oki and I had noticed while waiting for the bus. The buds will never open, he finally decided impatiently. Today they were in full bloom. Oki lay in his coffin.

Everything Was Wrong

If I had acted according to my faith, Oki's body would simply have somehow been laid in the earth, for worship of the dead is pagan. But a primitive emotion, not my faith, made the decision here, and from the man in black I ordered the most expensive coffin, the most beautiful roses, and had I been able, I would have built Oki a tomb to hold everything he had loved. I felt like a pagan: funerary offerings as a last symbol of my tenderness toward him and for his pleasure on his long journey. I would have dressed him in his flannel trousers and the leather jacket that was his favorite.

It was a completely normal first-class burial, and I went through all the stages of torture required by our ceremonies over a dead body.

First, the coffin in the chapel. Closed it was even more ugly. Within this shell Oki was lying with my rose.

Second, the organ playing "Commit Thou All That Grieves Thee," Oki's favorite hymn. For a brief moment it brought me joy, but then the melody destroyed my composure. It was a dangerous moment; I did not want to be overcome by emotion, but to think clearly. According to God's promises, Oki is now alive in another form of existence, according to God's will. Faith is calm. I clung to the quiet words of the chaplain. They offered me support.

Third, the coffin is picked up. Six men wearing grotesque hats bear it away.

Fourth, the walk to the grave. Why do we go so slowly, like a theatrical procession?

Fifth, the open grave. Earth — rich, red earth. Earth thou art, to earth thou shalt return. How simple. I had purchased a double plot, and someday a grave of equal size will be dug alongside for me, and then I will lie next to Oki. Thus I have a sense of order, and of the earthly termination of a shared life, after which our bodies even in death will lie together and waste away, if no war disturbs the earth and disinters our corpses. Someone hands me roses. I toss them on the coffin; soon they will be buried. Someone hands me a shovel; the earth cascades over the flowers. For a dead body, so many dead flowers. I should have realized and prevented it.

Sixth, I look around; a long row of people are standing there. Someone had told me I didn't have to stay. Perhaps I would offend the people, who were already beginning to toss clods of earth and extend their hands to me, if I went away. I didn't care. I suffered, here and everywhere.

The final torture: conversation after the burial.

Now I know how I should have buried Oki: no obituaries, no black clothes, no flowers, no grotesque hats, no strangers at his grave, no conversation afterward. Death was something between God, Oki, and me. Everything was wrong that diverted me from that course.

The Organizer

My new life began with a desk organizer. Irene had brought it when everyone had taken his departure after the burial, and chaos was left behind. Oki would have laughed and said, "What a mess you've made of my immaculate home!"

Irene had realized that it would torture me to rummage through Oki's papers, where I would see his handwriting everywhere, and she began to sort everything into that desk organizer, arranging everything neatly by subject. It was she who got out our will, saw to the death certificate, notified the company, and had payment made to me. She took me along whenever something had to be signed, and I placed my signature where I was shown. Without a word she carried out for me what each new day demanded, and after burial the daily round is not devoted to emotions, but to documents and officials. It seems ridiculous to set down the details, but every life must have regularities, and that desk organizer became the basis of order for me.

The Straits of Fear

"And this transition from a familiar existence to another of which we have not the slightest knowledge is something so violent that it cannot take place without convulsing the lives of those who remain behind" (Goethe).

Oki was on his way to God; every moment took him further and further from me. I remained behind in the straits of fear, as the book of Job puts it. The straits of fear, not because God was distant, but because ever since Oki's death he was so terrifyingly near. Formerly men veiled their faces in the presence of God. They did so, I now felt, out of terror, not symbolically, like the modern empty gesture.

Now Oki stood much closer to God than I. Was he, too, even more than I, in the straits of fear? Or was he reaching the realm of bliss, as he had written in a variant of the verse he had learned for confirmation: "What does it profit a man if he gains the whole world, when bliss begins only after death?"

The few Bible passages that deal with Hell now burned within my soul. When one is happy, Paradise seems within an arm's reach and Hell very distant, something one reads about occasionally without really caring. What gave me the right to believe Hell did not exist?

Now Oki could subtract nothing from his life, add nothing to it. Was he now rendering account "for every single word"? A terrible phrase, which I would always have preferred to gloss over. The rich man before whose door Lazarus lay had certainly never killed or robbed anyone, he had presumably never borne false witness, had perhaps never committed adultery, had honored his parents, had perhaps even professed his faith in God, and only overlooked poor Lazarus at his door because he was enjoying life — and he was "in the torments of Hell." Who might escape Hell? A terribly small number, as men once believed? The majority, as a more liberal age hoped? Everyone, by the simple expedient of eliminating Hell?

Confronted with the enormity of the word "Hell," it does not matter whether we picture it in garish colors, separated from Paradise by a great gulf, a place like that depicted by Hieronymus Bosch is his *Garden of Earthly Delights,* or follow the enlightened tradition of considering it a condition. For Luther, Hell seems to have been the bad conscience of the spirit, but only until the Last Judgment, when man "will be cast into real bodily Hell," body and soul. Teilhard de Chardin accepts Hell with a kind of uneasiness: "O Jesus, master of terrible beauty and jealousy, I shut my eyes to what my human weakness cannot yet understand and therefore cannot yet bear, the fact that there are people who are damned."

I, too, wanted to shut my eyes to what I could not bear and yet pursued me — except that it was not Jesus I implored, but God. After Oki's death I made a clear distinction between my prayers to God and my prayers to Jesus. Death, Hell — these were in the hands of God, before whom I stood in terror, not of Jesus; but God had sent us Jesus, so that we should not be dashed to pieces against him.

Later whenever I spoke the word "Hell," people responded, depending on whether or not they believed in its existence, with embarrassed or indulgent smiles, as though I had touched on something improper. We exclude Hell from our daily lives, just as we exclude death. But I know only that I was afraid for Oki. Had he died bearing the burden of guilt — I do not mean the thousand venial transgressions that we all commit — had he died bearing the burden of guilt, I should never have been able to escape the straits of fear.

After the burial, my panic fear subsided. It was as though Oki had reached his destination, the place that Jesus had prepared for him. In the book of Job we also read: "For God will also tempt you forth from the straits of fear into a broad place, where there is no affliction."

The Identity Card

Irene handed in Oki's identity card for me. She went in to see the official while I waited on a wooden bench in the corridor. Oki was dropped from the list of men on earth. I would have wanted to scream, simply to scream irrationally. Edvard Munch painted a picture, *The Scream*, that long haunted me as a child: a bridge in the background, a woman in front of it, her hands pressed to her head, eyes wide with terror. Now I am struck how often the psalmist screams.

How intense his faith must have been, allowing him to scream! But who screams to God today? An office is not the place for screaming; it is the place where people are entered in lists and dropped from lists, silently.

My God, my God, where is Oki now? There, where Jesus has prepared a place for him. I believe it, and I believe that I shall see him again. But now, now I want to have him!

Nature's Terror

"Without Jesus Christ death is dreadful; it is nature's abomination and terror" (Pascal). I was like a piece of red-hot iron on the anvil, held by tongs and being beaten, stroke upon stroke, into a form I did not want.

Herodotus records that the Trausi buried their dead amid joy and laughter because they had escaped all evils and now lived in happiness and bliss.

Jesus Sirach is more gentle: "Mourn over the dead, for his light is gone out; but mourn not overmuch, for he is at rest." And Luther: "God wishes us to mourn, but our mourning is to be moderate and not too great; the belief in eternal bliss is to work comfort in us."

How men must struggle to achieve a natural relationship with death! Formerly it was not considered blasphemous to represent life as a dance of death, to depict men and women as skeletons in brocade, to incorporate death frantically into life, to luxuriate in bodily decay and spiritual horror as though life were only a single nightmare before death. Today we seek no less frantically to exclude death from everyday life and render it innocuous. How difficult it is neither to disregard death nor to pay it exaggerated respect, but simply to accept it as the will of the God in whom we trust. Throughout millennia, every epoch, bearing the stamp of its own religion and culture, has sought its own relationship with death, and in every epoch the individual must struggle to achieve his own relationship with death.

"Mourn not overmuch" — that is the path man has slowly come to take, very slowly, and it is undoubtedly the right path. Boundless joy, boundless mourning, overwhelm nature and undermine faith. In a letter of consolation, Luther writes: "We pray to God that he may comfort your flesh, for the spirit has cause for rejoicing." This probably represents the dichotomy: for the flesh, death is "nature's terror"; for the spirit, it is joy. Pascal goes on: "In Jesus Christ, death is quite different; there it is sacred, and the joy and love of him who believes." From abhorrence to joy over death — how could such a change take place without an inner convulsion?

Things Survive

A senseless rage gripped me: Oki was no longer there — his hat was hanging in the closet. The things he had left behind survived as though to mock me, and I was afraid to touch them, as though they might burn my fingers.

Irene relieved this new torment. She quietly assembled all those things and placed them in Oki's closet. When she shut the door, I took refuge in my room. Only Oki's walking sticks would remain in the copper bucket by the entrance, a small silent symbol that this had been and would remain our home; I also kept his keys to the house on their awkward long chain. Later one can have a tender affection for these little things that belonged to a person one loved; at first they are an unbearable torment.

It was weeks before Oki's last belongings were locked away. Something of his would repeatedly turn up — his napkin ring in a drawer that I hadn't opened, his dirty laundry in the hamper, his shaving lotion in the medicine cabinet — and every unexpected encounter meant a new struggle for me, because these small things still bore his stamp.

Once again, it took a long time before I could open Oki's closet to arrange the things Irene had laid inside or I had later tossed inside in panic. I gave his personal effects away to people who lived far away, out of fear of seeing his clothing on another man.

It does not matter whether one leaves his things untouched, turning his home into a mausoleum, to the amusement of many, or bitterly obliterates all traces, or holds on to only a few things like a fetish — it is the same wretched attempt on the part of everyone who mourns to make his suffering less unbearable. To determine what to do with the things does not lie within our will; the decision takes place within us, and we must follow its lead.

Jesus Wept over Death

Each time despair overtook me, this passage from the raising of Lazarus comforted me. Jesus did not despise the suffering of those who mourn. Jörg Zink renders freely: ". . . then he was seized by anger at man's old enemy, death . . ." However one may translate and interpret this passage, Luther says plainly, "Jesus' eyes overflowed," and most English translations say simply, "Jesus wept." Where Jesus wept, I might suffer; he who had become man knew what I suffered. I did not need words in my defense; I needed only to say, "Lord, you know what I suffer; come, help me." Here I was consciously addressing Jesus; I might beg him for relief. To God I dared only say, "Your will be done."

It nevertheless long continued to sting me when a friend would write that she had thought faith made death easier to bear. I was upset until, reading in the Bible that our pastor had given us at our wedding, I found, among many other notes Oki had made, a quotation from a devotional passage: "Faith offers no protection against anxiety and sorrow, but faith offers security in anxiety and sorrow." Indeed, that was my experience; I suffered, I suffered no less than any nonbeliever, but I suffered within the security of God.

Going to Church

The first time I went to church there was no one to go with me. I suspected what was awaiting me, but still did not want to delay going any longer. The organ intensified my torment, and the sermon had nothing to say to me; my sorrow was stronger than the words of the preacher.

In front of the church stood groups of people talking to each other. I went past them and returned home; no one could be lonelier than I. Later I discovered that it was good thus; in church everyone stands alone with his pain and his hope in the presence of God, even when he is with others.

Should We Pray for the Dead?

There was no question for me to ask; I *had* to pray for Oki. Day after day I prayed to God: "Bless him, hold him in your loving hands." I turned to God however I happened to be feeling, and thus found a kind of peace in my need. Only later, when I was once again capable of thinking, was I concerned over whether I ought to pray for Oki.

I knew that Luther had said, ". . . when you have prayed once or thrice, you should believe that you have been heard, and you should cease to pray, lest you tempt or mistrust God." Luther is probably referring here to the prayer that God will redeem the soul: "Pray thus: Dear God, if the soul is in such state as it may still be aided, I beseech you show your mercy upon it; and when you have prayed thus once or twice, let be, and entrust the soul to God." In the period before the burial, while I was in "the straits of fear," I besought God to redeem Oki, as Luther describes here. If Luther so firmly forbade further prayers as being intercession for the dead, it was probably because ever since the time of Augustine the notion of purgatory as a temporary place of purification had become more and more widespread, and prayers for the shortening of the torments suffered by the dead had come to assume increasing importance.

Today, years later, my daily prayer for Oki is not a petition of this sort. I prayed that God would protect him as long as he was on earth beside me; why should I not continue to pray that God will bless him merely because he is in another realm of God? Since Oki was summoned home by God, I pray for him and for the host of those called home, that God may bless them, in his good time reuniting us all at the end. This prayer is for me a point at which I feel linked through God with all those I love, here on earth or already in the next world. Every day this prayer gives me peace, joy, and strength. What could be wrong with prayers that God has neither commanded nor forbidden?

The Date

I did not read the paper, I did not listen to the news; I stood apart from the events of the world about me. For me there was only the time before Oki's death and after Oki's death. Things happened before or after his death. I saw people before or after his death; the details of my life grouped themselves about this point. This caesura in time seemed to me to have no beginning, no end, like eternity. I became calm in my torment. Was I experiencing, as Teilhard de Chardin describes it, that "God must hollow us out and empty us in order to penetrate within us"? As the torment lessened, I lost the sense of eternity. Time embraced me once more, with dates, deadlines, and plans.

Sometimes I long to go back to this point at which I suffered unbearably but stood on a threshold where I could have been transformed. In every grief, I think, a person grows toward some time beyond himself, because he is touched by God. Was I at that time, to change the Augustinian phrase about man's "happy fault," living in the happiness of grief?

LIFE WITHOUT HIM

Alone in Our House

The first day alone in our house I spent wandering irresolutely about, as though my restlessness could break the stillness surrounding me. How often Oki's baritone had filled the rooms with sound, now humming, now intoning a song parlando. In vain I listened for the sound of his voice; I was alone.

"Love me, as at the end of all things I see nothing better than to love you and to live with you," Goethe wrote to Christiane Vulpius. As mature individuals, finding each other after sorrow, Oki and I, too, had found nothing better. Among the entries in Oki's notes for his memoirs I found: "B. introduces me to Liliane. We marry. We love each other and are happy." It had been as simple as that! In another of Goethe's letters to Christiane, we read: "There is really nothing better than loving and being together." Nothing is worse than the separation that follows.

Exhausted by my continuous pacing, I wanted to rest. Perhaps in Oki's room — where I saw his chair, with the arm over which he usually draped a leg and the spot where he would usually rest his head when he looked over to see me sitting on the sofa. Or should I lie down in my own room, where he would never again dash in, excitedly interrupting my rest with some inspiration, and at the same time being careful so as not to fall over my fragile French armchair? I was unable to go to sleep because I was afraid to wake up. I could not read, because the letters would have danced meaninglessly before my eyes. I had to lie there and suffer.

The first day alone — is that correct? Surely God is present! One often ignores his presence when one has another's company, but at any second he can take from our side that person we love. *The only sure thing is always God's presence.* It seemed to me as though God was audible in my silence; I was no longer alone.

Phone Conversations

When the telephone rang through the silence of the first day, it was like the breaking of a magic spell. I ran to the phone. It was Verena. From then on she called me every morning and every evening through the first days. If people only knew how much they could help by merely calling! To hear the sound of someone else's voice and my own was a deliverance and a gift on lonely evenings. I lift up the receiver, drawn as though by magic, and this tiny movement brings new life flooding into me.

Even during the first night without Oki a phone call interrupted for a moment the charmed circle of grief in which I was imprisoned; from another continent the voice of my stepson was suddenly in the room, and the solicitous sound of his words contributed to my relief.

Gravestones

When Oki and I used to take the O bus, which went past the cemetery, we would see the widows with their flowers getting off there. Oki felt sorry for this company, and had often told me he did not want me to observe any funerary cult at his grave. I have never had any particular feeling toward graves, but when I failed to receive approval for Oki's gravestone with the familiar baroque lantern that he had loved, I put up a bitter fight, much to my astonishment. According to my beliefs, the gravestone should have meant very little to me.

I did not want a cross for Oki. Only for someone who had died in Christ's behalf would I perhaps venture to set up a cross at the grave — a very small cross. It was during the Middle Ages, which were much possessed with death, that people began adding names to crosses and setting them up as gravestones. But the dead need not the cross but the resurrection, for the last word is not the agony of the cross but the joy of the resurrection! What symbol is there for the resurrection? When people began to decorate tombs with the figure of the departed, who was often depicted lying down with a footrest so that he would appear to be standing, open eyes and youthful features were meant to suggest the hope of resurrection. Thus on an English tomb Sir Ralph Greene and his wife await the Second Coming hand in hand, their eyes open — a lovely monument! On tombs of married couples one sometimes finds the husband with his feet resting on a lion, the symbol of strength, the wife with her feet upon a dog, the symbol of faithfulness.

What a range of emotions is recorded in the structures made for the dead — from the pyramids, embodying a titanic will to survive, to the ossuary of the monks on Mount Athos, where the bones of the dead, having lain three years in the earth, are simply piled high because death is so unimportant. The Greeks, with their sense of proportion, for a time opposed exaggerated funerary luxury and would permit only simple structures. In the case of our Christian graves and tombs, the emotion probably ranges from carelessness to ostentation, from tender restraint to crudity or embarrassment: monuments where decay is hideously depicted in terms of worms that invade the corpse, toads that crawl over the face; monuments with skeletons and skulls; monuments with saccharine marble angels or even a sweetly sleeping girl; irregular blocks of stone carved into meaningless shapes, saying nothing.

And the inscriptions! Today it is not our desire to praise our dead on their monuments, to ask the prayers of passersby in their behalf, or to chisel sentimental poems on stone; but why have we become so sterile and so unnatural in our form of expression? Does it always have to be Bible passages? Does not the simple phrase *a demain* ("until tomorrow") on a pedestal express radiant faith and love? Or the almost joyous words on a gravestone in the old cemetery at Freiburg: *la première au rendez-vous* ("she came first to our rendezvous") – that was appropriate for us, except that Oki got there first!

Today I am more generous in my thoughts about stones and inscriptions. I had my way with the wrought-iron lamp, but the stone is a failure.

Strange, these trips to the cemetery, to God's acre—these trips in the rain, in snow, in sunshine, and always in torment. No, not always! Today I am disconcerted, standing between Oki's silent neighbors; he is so alive to me that I am forced to ask at his grave why I decided to come here. Jeremias Gotthelf writes: "It is in life that I found my loved ones once more, not in the grave. I know that they can see me; whatever I do, whatever I engage in, they are there . . ." In God's acre it is the seed, which will spring up from the earth, that matters, not the stones on top!

Lonely Meals

Don't forget to eat! Those were the words with which Oki had often laughingly interrupted our conversations. I could no longer sit at the table where I had sat with him. I would have had to stare at the place across from me that he had filled with his broad shoulders, where specks of dust now danced before me.

After our first few meals together, which I began by saying grace, he had expressed surprise and asked whether I intended always to use the same lines – he expected me to use my own words. Struggling for words, learning to express my feelings more precisely, I discovered how to give thanks simply and truly.

When Verena found out that I had gotten used to gulping down a few bites at the corner of some table, she placed a small round table beside the window for me, from which I could see the tops of the trees. Later I turned on the news to outwit myself with pictures, so that I would not notice the place where no one was sitting across from me.

The World Beyond

"But such incomprehensible matters lie too distant to be the object of daily contemplation and thought-destroying speculations. A good man who intends to take his proper place in this world and is therefore called upon daily to strive, to struggle, and to work will let the future world take care of itself, being useful and active in this one" (Goethe).

That was just what I could not do: let the future world take care of itself. Oki was in this future world. I thought of him, I followed him — how could I do so without thinking at all of his world? When people are happy together upon earth, the other world remains a place that need not be pictured too precisely; when one loses one's companion, it is difficult not to seek after him in his new abode with eager inquiry. I wanted to assemble the fragmentary data about Oki's new world that are scattered through the "Good News," for why should I not be able to contemplate what God had recorded in the Book of books? I knew my Bible as well or poorly as anyone who has been reading it daily since childhood, and my purpose was frustrated at the very first passage. It is that account in which Jesus says to the thief on the cross, "Today you will be with me in Paradise," although Jesus "had gone down into Hell." Apparent contradictions in the Bible had never disturbed me before, because they appeared unimportant within the total context of the "Good News"; but in the desperation of my initial period of grief, all passages referring to Paradise or "Abraham's bosom" suddenly took on immense importance. Later my mind was set at rest by the explanation that during those three days Jesus was not in Hell as we often understand the word, but in the "realm of the dead."

And yet even when I assembled all the Bible passages dealing with that realm until the resurrection, there remained "a terrible mystery of the beyond" (Teilhard de Chardin). We smile at the Paradise garden of Fra Angelico or at statues that represent "Abraham's bosom" realistically as a place of redemption. We marvel at the *Garden of Bliss* of Hieronymus Bosch. But were those men any less fervent in their faith than we, and do not our enlightened intellectual concepts fail as wretchedly in the presence of this "terrible mystery" as the graphic images of primitive thought?

One thing is sure: Jesus promises us the good news of an eternal life in another realm of God. Is it presumptuous for me to think that this realm appears a tiny bit less distant from me, not because I have sought and found what God keeps concealed from us, but because I think of it every day and because Oki and more and more others that I love are awaiting us in this place of "rest" (Thomas Aquinas) and "refreshment" (Tertullian)? "Paradise is the name of the place where those who have died in the peace of God are assembled" (Schlatter). I have never found the notion of Paradise stated more simply or beautifully. Oki has found rest, and I am waiting, confident that I, too, shall be allowed to find rest in that place which is a stage in God's plan of creation.

The Magic of Suffering

For quite a while I thought I could no longer bear living in our home, which Oki had loved; I hated our dwelling place without him. When Mrs. C. was widowed, in a fit of despair she sold her house in Bordighera, moved to Rome, found the same agony there, and finally, overcoming all obstacles, repurchased her old house in Bordighera. Any widow can be pressed into such a crisis, which is only one of the many that are possible, even if she does not have the means to escape from her home. I stayed in our house, and now that I am no longer trying to escape from my grief, I feel protected there, because Oki had loved it. The magic of suffering!

When?

"The dead rest in the promise that they will rise again" (Luther). When will they rise again? What concerned me was not the *when* of the resurrection at the Second Coming after the refreshment and rest of Paradise, but the *when* of the new life now, following death. It bothered me that death until the resurrection is often compared to sleep. Luther speaks of death as a deep and sweet sleep; even Jesus says, "Lazarus is asleep." When does the state after death pass from sleep to waking consciousness? I could not evade this question, even though I knew that no human being, no world of books would ever be able to answer it for me.

There was the Bible passage saying that before Jesus' resurrection he was three days in the kingdom of the dead and that he preached to them. Did he preach to those who had not heard the message of salvation, or to those who had not accepted it, or to both groups, that all might be saved? I had always agonized over the fact that *we* had been permitted to experience the message of Jesus, unlike legions of men before Christ's birth, and afterwards, and even today. Were the three days the time when *all* God's creatures might hear the message, both in the past and in the future? For Jesus' words can no more be without effect in the kingdom of the dead than upon the earth! Did the three days Jesus spent in the kingdom of the dead have the same meaning for the departed as the three years of his ministry upon earth had for the living? In the eyes of God, time is nothing!

If Jesus preached to the departed — whoever they might be — in the kingdom of the dead, they must have heard his voice, and they cannot be conceived as "asleep" in the sense of slumbering. Jesus certainly did not spend his time with men asleep. I am thinking of an old picture representing Jesus as he preaches to the dead. Does this mean that the dead, like us on earth, await in their own kingdom the bliss of the Second Coming, when we shall all arise, but await their transformation without pain and without death, nearer to Jesus and to God? Does it mean they could pray for us?

No theologian or scientist will ever be able to say anything about the state of man after death. Why should we not simply accept the few Bible passages that deal with the subject? It is comforting to me and a source of joy: Jesus preached to the dead who were *not* asleep!

Going Shopping

My first shopping trip was a *via dolorosa* — the sympathetic expressions that I did not want to see, the well-meaning words of genuine concern that I did not like to hear, the tears that had to be repressed, the embarrassed silence between the words of sympathy, and the quarter-pound of butter that I finally had to ask for.

When I was standing outside once again I suddenly imagined that I was only pretending to be a widow, that Oki would soon be standing beside me, that he would take the bag and I would try to match his long strides, that he would brandish the umbrella over my head and I would get completely soaked and laugh and say once more that the only thing wrong with our marriage was getting drenched in the rain . . .

As I slowly wend my way home, I ask myself if self-pity is not insinuating itself into my grief. That would be a degradation of my sorrow. I must be careful and keep up my defenses: no self-pity!

Longing for the Beyond

Marie Luise Kaschnitz writes tellingly of being a widow: ". . . I knew what my distress was, this agonizing tension between the longing for death and the will to live . . ."

As long as Oki was with me, I was happy to live on this earth and felt no longing for the beyond. Now I know the danger of the tension between the longing for death and the will to live, but I must not long for the beyond only to be with Oki once more. This new force of longing can be a beneficent force that I should not lose, but it must first of all be the force of longing for God and Christ and for the kingdom of love where there is no more death or grief, the kingdom where Oki and the host of others will also be.

"May the Lord and supreme comforter Jesus Christ, who has claimed your son for himself and taken him from you, comfort you and strengthen you with his grace until the day when you will see him once again in eternal bliss. What unspeakable joy awaits us there, to which many others have preceded us, calling us every day and exhorting us and enticing us that we may follow" (Luther).

Longing to leave this earth, the place of sorrow, and come to another world, the place of comfort? Despite and in the midst of my longing for the beyond, I must *here* and *now* build a life that will be meaningful for me, even though I know it is transitory, and attempt to fulfill God's commandments at least in part.

The Person One Was

One can never become once more the person that one was. It is true, of course, and no cause for sorrow that at every moment in one's life one is a different person, body and soul, from the person one was the second before, but the transformation takes place gradually. The death of someone we love, however, transforms us suddenly.

"Come with me to my castle" — without Oki's enraptured expression, Don Giovanni will never delight me again. I shall never again be able to appreciate Japanese woodcuts if Oki does not hold them in his hands. I shall never again be enchanted by the glory of a spring or fall in our forests if Oki is not walking beside me, idly swinging his walking stick. I shall never again look forward to visiting one of my childhood haunts because I can no longer show it to Oki. He accompanies me everywhere, but he is not there. I look at everything through the glasses of grief, and they transform the familiar landscape. I see and hear as though I were a stranger to myself. The terrible longing for Oki and the eternal, agonizing refrain: never again, never again.

"It takes all the composure of my faith to accept what in its own right is really breaking my heart and attempt to transform it into a constructive element" (Teilhard de Chardin).

Dialogues at Night

Another evening of quiet; in the distance, through the branches of the trees, I see the lights of the houses going on and off.

I want the torment to stop! I could drink oblivion.... How simple, and who, stricken by grief, has not occasionally had this thought? A few glasses of wine — and I would cease to carry on this ghostly dialogue with Oki, in which I speak to him as I used to in our dialogues at night, but all in silence, as between the deaf and dumb. Drink oblivion? No! "If what we desire does not take place, then something better will take place" (Luther).

The silent dialogues at night brought me to the confident belief that I would show myself poor and weak if I were to end them out of cowardice.

I Cannot See His Name

A letter addressed to Oki arrived. It stung like a lash! The same day I had everything transferred to my name — the telephone, the gas, the electricity, everything. I could not bear seeing Oki's name, for *he* was no longer there. How long did letters continue to arrive addressed to him! "Please forward" was stamped on one. Each time, the same pang of grief.

A name exercises strange and magical power. But only one thing matters: in the eyes of God Oki is not a nameless creature. "But rejoice, for your names are written in heaven."

Taboos

My tenderest memories became the most agonizing. I tried to segregate them in my memory, unconsciously suspecting that I must not lose them forever precisely because they would later become a precious possession. Now they were taboos for me.

I could no longer bear the sound of singing; I locked up Oki's record cabinet with its opera albums and innumerable lieder that had turned so many evenings into celebrations for us. I avoided certain routes, such as the road over St. Michael's Hill to the spa, which I used to race down, coming from a visit to my sick mother, when I knew Oki was there and I could catch sight of him waving to me in the distance. The silver tray that he kept filled with baked goods for teatime I gave away.

Some great, some small, all involuntary taboos. With the passage of time they disappear, first one and then another — I do not know the date or the reason. Many will never go: I will never again have flower boxes on the balcony; Oki carried them down to the garden, singing, on his last morning.

What Cannot Comfort

Never try to comfort a widow by telling her that other women have lost not only their husband but their daughter or son as well. A woman in grief is like a burned-out building; grief cannot be changed to a former state — there is no way to burn ashes.

Why Me?

Even if I do not ask this question aloud, how dangerously it insinuates itself in silence and speaks itself in mute bitterness. To ask this would be to reproach God: What did *I* do to deserve this, I and not the woman next door? When Oki and I were happy together, did I ask, "Why me?"

I must not degrade the anguish of my grief by turning it into a punishment. Instead of asking God reproachful questions, I should listen; perhaps God is asking me, "How strong are you?" Luther says that when God tortures us, "he is at the door."

The Lifelong Monologue

The first time I had to call a repairman, I said, "*We* would like to have such-and-such done; that's the way *we* want it." How happy I had been to leave the egocentric, categorical "I" of the days before our marriage and come to the circumspect "we"! Will I ever be able to retrace my steps back to "I"? I try to say "my house"; it hurts and strikes me as a lie. Our marriage was an active dialogue. The inquiring "you" was tossed back and forth like a ball: What do you think? What would you like? What appeals to you? Each of us felt his way into the thoughts of the other and rejoiced in each new discovery.

Now I have to engage in a lifelong silent monologue, and yet sometimes I would like to scream. To have him ask me questions and ask him questions in return surrounded me with a shell of tenderness that now has shattered.

The Other Ring

As with everything else, we were honest about our wedding rings. Oki, who did not like rings, had taken his off after the ceremony; I continued to wear mine. To a woman this ring means more than to a man, and because I was happy I enjoyed showing it off. Now Oki's ring lies in its box. I did not put it on, as the custom is, not because he had only worn it briefly and it is strange to me, but because I am still Oki's wife, even if I shall never see him again on earth. Furthermore, I do not like the idea of labeling myself a widow by wearing a double ring.

Words to Fear

Marital status: "widow." Another lash. It took a long time for me to stop rebelling at the word. I refused to pronounce it, used circumlocutions, and avoided looking at it in writing.

"A widow in the full sense is one who is alone in the world," Paul writes to Timothy. This special, oppressive loneliness of a widow! One can learn what it means to be single or married in the full sense through both joy and suffering, to be a widow in the full sense only through suffering. But it is a suffering illuminated by the joy that has preceded!

"Dead" — a word of torture. I said instead "departed" — and deceived myself. On the day I was able to say the word "dead" without fear, it lost its brutality for me, and really came to mean Oki's departure for his home with God.

A Walk

The day came when I left the house without having someplace in particular to go — the church or the cemetery, offices or stores. I went for a walk, my first walk alone. That Sunday I met many couples. I had never noticed before how many couples one sees on Sunday. Most of them I knew, the way one knows the people in the part of town where one lives, without stopping to say hello. Some stared at me in such a way that I could read their thoughts: "She brought about her husband's death." Sympathetic glances were almost harder to bear. I avoided people's eyes; I was ashamed of being alone; I felt as though I were responsible for Oki's death. I recalled that my mother, when she was young, never wanted to take a walk alone. "People might take me for a widow," she used to say, as though there was something wrong with that. Without having experienced it herself, she felt it to be an inferior state. Her instinct was right; I felt stigmatized.

The beauty of nature caused me pain. The couples upset me. The older ones passed me, arm in arm, like victors passing by the defeated enemy, and I thought, "That's the way we could have been." Shame and anguish almost drove me back home. No, I must not be a coward. I would not run away as though trying to evade a punishment. I forced myself to keep on going. But after that I avoided taking Sunday walks, or I would walk quickly as though I were expected somewhere, or I would go out late when there were no other people to meet.

With the passage of time I regained my confidence and suffered less. Now I could feel sympathy not only for myself but also for the couples I met, and I thought, "One of you will also walk alone someday; you do not realize yet the anguish that awaits one of you."

Now I go out again even on Sunday, alone or in company, however it happens. I have always borne whatever was God's will: being single, married, widowed. "Whatever befalls you, that is God's will; rely on that and lay aside your care" (Tersteegen).

The Intermediate State

Since I have held daily converse with a man who is dead, I no longer stand entirely within this life. I am in an intermediate state, looking for a new orientation. In this intermediate state life on earth takes on a different meaning, and converse with one who is dead gives a remarkable strength: the daily routine no longer matters so much; its importance derives only from its end. It is as though the departure of the person one loved caused the realities of this life to lose their importance, and life after death acquired reality in equal measure. Existence on earth becomes like a dream in which one suddenly realizes that one will awaken with death, and only then will one be truly alive.

In this intermediate state, although still active in life, one approaches death serenely, and the joy is greater than the grief. Zschokke writes of a man whose friends were trying to divert and cheer him up after the death of his wife and children: "Don't bother! Sadness is the farthest thing from my mind; in fact, I am more profoundly happy than ever before. Now I live in two worlds. My wife and my children belong to me always and everywhere, and I to them. I beseech you, don't amuse yourselves at my expense; don't comfort me!"

If He Knew . . .

If Oki knew that I feel too dizzy to get up in the morning, that my father must undergo a serious operation, that I cannot find a nurse to relieve me in caring for my mother . . . I must not fall into this whining litany. This "if Oki knew" will be with me to my death, but it must be nothing more than a thought I must learn to smile at, to smile happily because God gave me Oki and because I am coming nearer to him every day. Jesus died to bring us *good* news, not sadness.

The First Guests

My first guest forced me to lay aside my grief in order to bring joy to someone else. For his visit I had to decorate the room with flowers, prepare the food he liked, look for the book that would please him. Every step that led me away from myself and toward others was painful — for how happy we had been, entertaining our guests together! — but brought healing. I learned to bear Oki silently within me, and discovered that everything that detached — nay, released — me from myself brought me more profoundly and joyfully to him. "Therefore grieve so as also to take comfort, for you have not lost him but sent him on ahead, to be received into eternal bliss" (Luther).

Speaking of Him

At the outset I could speak only of Oki; nothing else meant anything to me, and what other people said was nothing to me but noise. There are women whose mouths are sealed against the happiness of the past. I had thought I was one of them. How little one knows about oneself! Did I want to talk about Oki in a desperate attempt to set him among the living and keep him alive in the memory of those who had been his friends? But I also talked about Oki to people who had never known him and were strangers to me. On such occasions I felt insecure, because these new acqaintances meeting me without Oki got to know only a part of me. I desperately kept saying "we" when I talked, as though to make manifest that I was only one member of a couple, even if he, the other member, would never again stand beside me.

For those on the outside, how small may be the distance separating grief from the grotesque. Have not I myself smiled over those widows who speak of "their" dead husband? I had to learn not to talk about Oki. A dead man becomes our property in a way the living never could.

One Might

The point comes where one might begin afresh. One is outwardly free; one might undertake gymnastics or buy new clothes, open a store, enroll in a university, write a book, do volunteer work — one might, but one does not. One is free and feels constrained. Constrained by God? Constrained by the departed loved one? A process is reaching its critical point, and what is being born needs time; one must wait.

Alone on the Platform

I was going to visit friends, and stood alone on the platform. It was the platform where Oki and I had gotten out four years before;

ugly as it is, it had always seemed to us the most beautiful platform in the world. The last period of our life in the nearby miniature metropolis that we loved was to be our best. We did not envy young people; those who are mature enjoy their pleasures more intensively. We did not envy the rich; we had enough for our needs. In a house whose view delighted us afresh each day, no longer drained by the demands of earning a living, we could devote ourselves to the things that absorbed our attention. We were happy.

Now I was standing on this platform once more, for the first time by myself. My grief ached inside me; I felt as though I were being torn apart. I almost ran away. But where could I go? I could not escape from my agony — I bore it everywhere with me. But it seemed even more unbearable on this platform. The wind whistled about me, the tracks stretched endlessly in both directions, straight as an arrow through the plain. Alone in the solitude of another planet I could not have felt more lost. I had longed for the company of a happy family, and now my friends were waiting for me; I had to go.

The train pulled in. Carrying my suitcase I rushed past the nearest car so as not to have to watch how a man was carefully helping his wife aboard, so as not to have to hear how he gave her meaningless friendly reminders.

"O God, you knead me . . ." (Teilhard de Chardin).

NEW LIFE TAKES TIME

First Homecoming

It was a mercy that I did not realize how terrible the first home-coming after a trip without Oki would be. Arriving at the platform, where no one was waiting for me, I ran to the taxi as though pursued; I rushed up the steps to our apartment, opened the door — and stood aghast. A well-meaning friend had decked everything with flowers. The apartment was alive, and it seemed to me as though Oki had to come through every door to meet me, with his rolling gait and beaming smile. I collapsed on Oki's sofa; for the first time I broke into sobs.

"We should honor the dead, but not with tears and sighing; we should struggle and fight to live after their example, with strength and serenity" (Jeremias Gotthelf).

Now when I come back from a trip, I am grateful to Oki for having furnished me with the shelter of a home, and like the psalmist, I feel that "God brings home those who are alone."

Why?

Many a day I felt the gnawing question, Why? Magazines piled up on my desk, their call unheeded.

Earn money: why?

Dust: why?

Put flowers in vases: why?

Read: why?

Take care of myself: why?

Teilhard de Chardin says, "All conscious energy is, like love, grounded on hope." Because I had hope, I had to raise the energy — or I would have proved myself to be without faith and deceived myself.

There is no day of one's life that is without significance. There is only a day when one is happy, another when one suffers. In either case the content of each day is equally important: to keep active, in the hope that our activity, whatever it may be and minor as it may be, will contribute to God's creative plan. This "why," no longer a question, makes every activity meaningful and a source of joy. "Faith is not a perspective on the world, but a source of energy" (E. Spranger).

The Body Rebels

The next time I went to the doctor, the nurse told me she was happy to see me looking better each time, no longer a shadow as on my first visit. She was right, but she gave me a start. My body was rebelling; it wanted the torture to stop, it wanted to grow strong. I was ashamed of myself; it seemed as though I were betraying Oki.

I do not know whether there is any truth to the tale that one horse will follow the other in death when they have long labored together in the harness; it is certainly true that a dog can follow his master in death. I made up my mind that such death of a living creature is the product of a pathetic but helpless drive. For the instinct of an animal, death may signify the end; for man it is a beginning. To follow another creature in death is the weakness of an animal; to continue to live is the strength of man. How weak are those widows who no longer care to live because they are no longer pampered and loved. It would have been deplorable and pagan to want to follow Oki in death. I must recover my health and do as much as God gives me strength to do, and as long as he gives me that strength. One must learn to deal with one's body; it serves us on the way to God.

Living Like Anna

The Bible tells us that Anna spent her life, having lost her husband after seven — only seven! — years, in prayer and fasting. Most English translations call her a "prophetess." Jörg Zink translates, "a favored woman." That struck me. I am not favored; I cannot live like Anna!

I had decided to live as a married woman; my marriage had been blessed by God and I had been allowed to cultivate it as a gift of God. I never found the life of Elizabeth of Hungary very convincing. It seemed to me that she should have been able to do good without going into seclusion and neglecting her family. But now Oki is no longer with me, I have been alone and free for years — and my conscience nags me. To Joseph, the husband of Mary, who is otherwise mentioned too sparingly, an angel appeared four times in a dream, bringing him commands from God, Matthew says. Today we no longer receive commands from God in our dreams, or we no longer perceive them; but is our conscience not one single command from God? If I were to follow my conscience, I would not, it is true, have to spend my life in prayer and fasting; but I would have to eliminate many incidentals and devote all my strength to service of my neighbor. That I cannot do; I cannot live like Anna!

"The material world is simply the mountain slope that one may just as well climb as descend" (Teilhard de Chardin). I am not descending, but I am also not climbing; I am remaining stationary, and that is bad. The story in the Bible about the rich young man who keeps the commandments but does not have the strength to sell everything he possesses in order to give to the poor has always upset me. Mark is the only evangelist who adds: "And Jesus looked at him and loved him." Even this man, who seemed worthy of love to Jesus, did not sell everything he had in order to follow Jesus, but went away with a heavy heart. If the end of the story did not contain a ray of hope, "Everything is possible for God," the rich young man and I, even though we keep the commandments, would be lost.

I would not have as much to give away as the rich young man; but what matters is not the sum one donates, but the disposal of *everything*. It is so much easier to believe in Christ than to be a Christian! In his history of civilization, Friedell calls this "perhaps the greatest dichotomy in the existence of men on earth." It lies in the disturbing question, What is the purpose of life, beauty or goodness? I know that it is goodness, but I cannot set beauty aside.

"I do not belong entirely to God, nor entirely to things" (Teilhard de Chardin). Of course, I perform my little coolie labors for the sick, the poor, the community. I work, but how much time and money do I still spend on what I find beautiful in nature, in art, and in our home instead of on what would be good? Beauty pricks my conscience. I shall not conquer the "mountain slope" like Anna, but I shall try with all my might to ascend at least a few steps. "The same material world that seemed to suggest to us greater pleasure and less effort now becomes a spur to enjoy less and make greater efforts" (Teilhard de Chardin).

He Would Have Said . . .

The first time Irene returned for a visit, I stood in the door and looked at her in despair. In my frantic attempt to find my footing, it occurred to me that Oki would have said, "Have fun, but think of me." Later Mrs. A., who was widowed many years ago, told me what she said to her sick husband once when he regretted that caring for him cost her so much effort: that, in turn, he should only grant her one request, to help her after he passed on. "And he does help me," she added simply.

The Books by My Bed

When a friend of mine was killed in the war, I found in a book Pascal's letter to his sister on the death of their father, and this letter helped me at a difficult time. Ever since then, Pascal has stood with a traditional translation of the Bible and a modern one, later joined by the paraphrase of Jörg Zink, on the table beside my bed. After Oki's death I discovered *The Divine Milieu* and letters by Teilhard de Chardin. For years the works of these two men of burning heart and cool spirit have been a source of constant joy to me.

Without a particular system, year in and year out I have let reviews or chance guide me to the works of great believers, and have thus built up a collection in my library. I could have built up a large selection of books beside my bed, from the Rule of Saint Benedict and the conversations of Brother Lawrence to the journals of Jochen Klepper. Pascal and Teilhard de Chardin suffice me for the final minutes or hours of each day. With them I am not alone. Every evening I am under the secure protection of God, just as Oki is.

The Eternal Home

When the heavens fall
and the end is come,
then we both will go
to the eternal home!

Oki wrote this in the Bible our pastor gave us when we were married. How did he hit on the phrase "eternal home"? How might he have pictured it? The only other place I have come across the expression is in Jochen Klepper, as the tile of his book on Katharina von Bora, the book he was unable to finish, which I shall always regret. "The eternal home" radiates such a sense of security. Has Oki already reached it? Now I must find the way alone.

The Month of the Dead

I love the month of the dead. My friends think they have to show more sympathy for me in November than at other times. They are wrong. In the spring months the flowers that Oki loved become claws to lacerate my heart. In the month of the dead I am calm and quiet, like nature; it is my month. I always think of Oki, and thus always of death; it is the gateway to my great happiness. Why should I fear the month of the dead?

Three Wishes

If Oki were still with me and I could have three wishes, as in a fairy tale, I know what one of them would be: to be able to die with him. The people in the fairy tale never thought of this, the most important wish for happiness on earth, and yet every loving couple is confronted with the anguish of death that will separate them, an anguish worse than any other. How does it happen that this wish is always forgotten?

"God keep you safe for me" was a line in a song that Oki used to sing. Today I would like to know all its lyrics, but I can no longer find them. It is true that I prayed daily for God to bless Oki, but I did not beseech him fervently to keep Oki safe for me, as a gift that might any second be torn from my grasp. Marriage, the most wonderful gift of God to man, is indissolubly linked with the horrible separation of death — as though God had to remind us that we are *his* creatures. Of course, the clergyman often alludes to this separation on the day of marriage. How beautifully the priest in Manzoni's novel says to the couple at their marriage that even a life unruffled by any disaster must end with great grief at the moment when they must part. "Love each other as traveling companions, with this thought, that your ways must one day part, and with the hope that you will meet again for all eternity." Every priest says it, many couples think of it, but no one can measure the terror of the separation until he himself suffers through it. And so death together will never be one of the three wishes in a fairy tale.

One, however, who was able to measure it, wrote a very different wish to his bride:

> If you are there, I'll go rejoicing
> To meet my death and find repose.
> How blissful then would be my dying,
> With your white hand upon mine lying
> And you to make my eyelids close.

A lovely song — a terrible wish. Johann Sebastian Bach was a widower when he wrote it; he had suffered the torment of separation from his beloved, and yet expected it of his second bride. For the most part it is men who make this wish. Our survival is the sacrifice we offer to our husbands.

Advent Sunday

On the first Sunday in Advent I missed communion at church. I had made my preparation and was disappointed. We are all God's living creatures, the departed and we, even though living in separate worlds. Through the Lord's Supper we are brought together, and thus I remain in association with Oki and all the rest. "A state consists of the living and the dead" (Winston Churchill). Well said! It had never before occurred to me that the number of the dead among whom I live is larger than the number of the living. If I were to add them up, the dead of history, my friends, and my family, how many there would be! And if I were to blot them out of my life along with all they have left me, what would remain?

The dead shape us.

His Tokens

It was many weeks before I could read a book again, and even then I shrank from the books in our personal library. I was afraid I would open a book and there find Oki's handwriting. He used to write something in every book he gave me so that later, when he was no longer with me, I would find tokens of him in all the books. The idea had made me happy, but I had smiled at his reason for it, since his family were all long-lived.

The joy of our marriage lay recorded in these lines he had impulsively jotted down. He had preserved everything: twice fourteen birthdays, fourteen Christmases, fourteen wedding anniversaries, holidays, events minor and major, illnesses, guests — even a bravely borne tooth extraction was mentioned with a touch of humor. On our first anniversary, by way of exception, I had written something myself: "November 23 finds us without regrets." From then on Oki had entered in this book an account of the state of our marriage; his last statement read: "Time has still not changed our happy state."

The time of shrinking from these entries is past. Now I sit in Oki's room during the evening and watch the lights of the houses blink on and off in the distance. Before, Oki had closed our old-fashioned wooden shutters in the evening, and then began our quiet hours, in which we were alone with our happiness. I could not move the heavy shutters by myself, nor do I have any happiness to hide now; but I have found peace. Now I look forward to my evenings alone with a book and Oki's entries. They furnish me with what he expected them to: tender, thankful memories.

Poverty of Language

A dead body means a body without life; but the dead live! This imprecision or, to me, falsity of language always bothers me. Perhaps there are theological, philosophical, linguistic discussions of it. I am only surprised that it does not seem to bother anyone in the course of everyday life. For centuries there has been no special word granted the dead who are alive. Is it a sense of this lack that led people to coin the lovely term "departed"? Is this why I refused for so long to speak of Oki as being "dead," because for me he was alive? Only in Lessing, with his crystal-clear mind, did I find any comment on this situation: "...and it is only to be ascribed to the poverty of language that it uses one and the same word to refer to both these states, the state that leads inescapably to death and the state of death itself." And in Bachofen I read: "Human language is too impoverished to clothe in words the wealth of ideas conjured up by the alternation of death and life, and those higher hopes that the initiate harbors." Especially about death should we not think precisely?

No Time

There is a story that Goethe's wife, at the hour of her death, sent a visitor away with the words, "Goethe's wife has no time today, she is busy dying." Today we have time for everything except for dying. Few people master the art of dying as well as the aged mother of Dr. K., who pushed her medicine away and said calmly, "I have lived until now; now it is time to die." Such dying must be learned. Life: a course with death as the final examination.

The First Christmas with Charles Dickens

On Christmas morning I had brought Oki my present, a little lantern with a candle. At the cemetery I tried to light it in the wind, saying to myself, "No self-pity." On this first Christmas I received no embrace, no present from Oki, nothing to make me happy, and yet everything: the birth of Christ. This Christmas I observed not to receive presents but to thank Christ. It was my first real Christmas.

Verena and Carl had invited me over for the evening with some other guests; as is true everywhere where people decorate their houses with choice art objects, the Christmas decorations, the candles, the brocade angels looked a bit lost in the room. After the Christmas carols on the record, we spoke of much, but not of the birth that had brought us together. For me it was nevertheless a festival of Christ; Verena and Carl surrounded me with their friendship, and wherever a gift is given with love, there is the brightness of Christmas.

On the way home I walked between two of the guests, a chemist and a physiologist, both of whom said they could not be believers because they were "scientists." As though Pascal and Teilhard de Chardin had not been scientists, and as though some limited science of this world could ever impugn the limitlessness of God! Just as I cannot prove to anyone that God exists, no one can prove to me that he does not.

Why did my friends feel sorrier for me on Christmas Eve than at other times, why had Verena embraced me especially lovingly as I left, if nothing special took place at Christmas?

I thought of Oki, for whom Jesus had prepared a place. At home there were no holiday decorations, no lights; when one is alone, one does not light candles. I read from a story by Charles Dickens and found him full of strength in the bearing of suffering. Ever since then I have read one of his works at Christmas; throughout the entire year I look forward to the quiet evenings. Christmas was always light to me. I was both sad and happy, like one "having nothing and yet possessing everything," as Paul writes. I was happier than those two guests who had accompanied me; I had heaven before me and they had nothingness.

Daily Portions

When I married, I had for many years made a practice of reading the daily portions of Scripture, which someone had once pointed out to me, and I brought them to Oki also at the beginning of each year.

We read them separately and rarely discussed them. But now and then a verse would excite Oki because it was appropriate to us or our friends or the situation, and he would rush in and recite it to me with passion.

On the first anniversary of Oki's death, the portions were: "I shall walk before the Lord in the land of the living," and "This is the promise that he has promised us, eternal life." Coincidence, of course, but what comfort on this dreaded day!

His Birthday

Oki's birthday is approaching. If I let my faith guide my thoughts, the day of his birth was a birth that leads to death, but the day of his death a birth that leads to life. Today I am happy, strangely happy. Memories of our life together surround me with silent joy, and the future stands before me with God's immeasurable promise. I have found a happiness that no one and nothing can take from me — except God himself. "... whether we esteem and love his will even more than our own selves, and all that he has given us to love and have upon this earth ..." (Luther). I feel as though I were coming unhurriedly but at an increasing pace toward the fulfillment of my hope.

Old Clothes

It had been difficult for me to put on mourning; it was almost more difficult to stop wearing it. Now I was attached to the black dress in which I had suffered through all the stages of my agony, and I did not want to pack it away. In its distinctive black I had felt cramped, as in a suit of armor, but it also frequently offered me protection. Wrapped in black and grief I was hardly aware of people and things in the city, and no one would have dared to approach me with trivialities. When I felt the tears coming on the street and I was helpless to restrain them, I would even have liked to hide behind that heavy widow's veil that had earlier seemed so theatrical to me. Later I was shocked to note the large number of women who were themselves dressed in mourning, who crossed my path with unseeing eyes.

Now it was no longer black that offended me, but color, and if I had been rich I would have given away all the bright clothing I had worn earlier. Suddenly to see it all again seemed unbearable, for each dress was associated with memories. The brown dress that I wore on the last evening we entertained a guest still had the brooch on its collar where Oki had pinned it for me.

More Love

Since Oki is no longer with me, I have found more love for others. I do not love him any less, but he is like someone who has gone on a trip and no longer has to be looked after. I have my time and my energy free for others. The people who are close to me now are at a greater distance than the man with whom I was one.

Today I am equally prepared for all, because they are all God's creatures. In my mother's room at the hospital I often gave sick strangers a drink, wiped their forehead, or performed one of the many ridiculously tiny services that they needed. There was not much else I could do, but there was some love in each tiny act, and I could sense that the sick felt my sympathy behind the banal gestures. They made me touching presents, and said kind things to me, even at the end, when they could hardly speak. To love all men for their own sake and not for my sake no longer seems too difficult now, and I have learned that one can also find happiness in this kind of love.

The Swifts

The swifts are back. With a shrill cry one of them streaks by my head, and I run in off the balcony. It had been one of our games: Who would be the first to see them in the spring?

A girl next door is practicing the piano, playing the theme from the Maigret series on television, which Oki was always so eager to turn on. I shut the window.

A man passes me on the street; I smell the colonge Oki used, and hurry to escape.

It is always too late to escape. Our emotions react so much more quickly than our thoughts! Even years later there will be pictures, melodies, odors that, even before I am consciously aware of them, resurrect my grief with a precision to which I must fall victim. There is no switch to turn off this automatic response. But now I no longer try to escape my grief, which I have day by day surrounded with a web of tenderness, that it may find ease. Now I let the swallows fly around me on the balcony; when that theme is played I no longer close the window; and when I breathe in that scent, I smile and continue on my way.

. . . For Time and Eternity

For a little while I have been haunted by fragments of a song with the words "I'll love you for time and eternity." These words, which meant nothing to me earlier, which I may have found old-fashioned, occurred to me years later without any apparent reason; I was struck by them. They reflect my feelings clearly, simply: Oki is in my heart for time and eternity. Now the seven little words are a comfort to me. Grief has its own standards, which should never be met with an indulgent smile.

A Wedding Next Door

One of their daughters is getting married. The terrace is hung with garlands of Chinese lanterns, music is playing through the open windows, groups of people are walking in the garden. I stand at the window; I must learn to view the happiness of others without bitterness.

A year later. The bride's father died suddenly. Now the other woman stands at the window, dressed in black. The grip of death, which has eased for me, is beginning to tighten on her. How good that she does not know the torments that await her.

How quickly men leave this earth! When we moved in, every evening we saw an old woman alone in one of the rooms; she kept the shutters open, left the light burning, and sat through the night at a round table. We felt pity for the unknown woman; she was sick and lonely. Soon she died.

Now still other people live next door, another couple. What awaits them? A wedding? A funeral? How short the period of grace between the two is! And we always live with insatiable appetite, as though there were no limit set to our lives.

NIGHT IS AS BRIGHT AS DAY

Grief Comes and Goes When It Will

On the anniversary of Oki's death, Verena had called me up early in the morning. She had spoken in a soft, husky voice, and tried touchingly to say the right thing. That morning — I do not know why — had not been one of the agonizing ones. It was rather one of those days on which I could be almost happy; like Ecclesiastes, I felt that "the day of death is better than the day of birth." Oki was delivered, and I was waiting for my deliverance.

At first my pain and grief revived each day at the hour of Oki's death, and it was a long time before I could get through that hour without feeling terribly upset. My anguish might erupt again tomorrow like a volcano and bury me under a lava of red-hot grief. Repeated experience, even now that I am composed, has taught me: grief comes and goes when it will. It springs from depths within us that we cannot plumb. Against it one is defenseless; one must be grateful when it subsides, resigned when it comes.

Work

When I set to work again on my scholarly articles, I had second thoughts, for I did not need the money. But there is no such thing as evil money, only money used for evil purposes, and it does not matter whether a widow employs her energy to work without pay for the benefit of society or to benefit society through the money she has earned. Paul puts it concisely: "Let each one remain before God as he was called." I think work is necessary for a widow, if she is not using it as an anesthetic but performs it meaningfully according to her ability. "To the perfection of creation we contribute through even the lowliest work of our hands. This is ultimately the significance and reward of our activity" (Teilhard de Chardin). Only faith, not work, can relieve the pain of our grief; but we need an activity to develop and perfect us according to God's will.

The High Seas of Life

I had kept putting it off like a mountain to be climbed, but I knew that I would have no peace until I had sorted through Oki's memoirs, to the extent that he had edited them. The last page that he wrote he had read aloud to me on the day before he died. His enthusiasm was contagious, and now, as I transcribed them, his voice pursued me. I could still hear how he had stressed a word, I knew the pauses when he would look at me expectantly . . . Each page was a torture.

"On the High Seas of Life" was to be the title of his memoirs, for he had often had to cross the seas between Alexandria and Tokyo, losing his Egyptian homeland in the First World War, his Japanese in the Second. These memoirs will remain unfinished. But what matters in the eyes of God is not the finished work, not a man's success, but his efforts.

Our late marriage had been for a short span of time a life raft for both of us, on which we had been allowed to rest. God has tossed us into the sea once more; he has Oki secure in his protection, I must still fight the waves until God's hand reaches out for me.

Not to Live in Avoidance of Grief

Goethe wrote to Schiller after the death of his child: "In such cases one does not know whether one does better to surrender oneself naturally to grief or to pull oneself together with the aids our civilization offers. If one decides on the latter course, as I always do, the improvement is only momentary; and I have noticed that nature again and again asserts her rights through new crises."

I did not have the choice that Goethe describes. In the first days of my grief I could not have accepted "the aids our civilization offers" even if I had wanted to; I could neither read nor listen to music nor look at pictures. I was separated by a curtain from the people and the things of this earth. Later I could have allowed myself to be diverted; it would have been an escape. It seems to me that whether one bears one's grief in faith or unbelief, one must learn not to avoid it but to live with it. Grief works at us, it makes us stronger day by day, because we cannot lean on those we love for support; it makes us freer, because we are alone with God. Suppressing grief would spoil us. Now, after many years, it is almost as though I could love my grief; at any rate it is no longer an enemy that I must fight, but rather it has become a part of me, has done more to shape me than any happiness ever has. Was I not in a way happy in my grief, because in the midst of my anguish I was thrown into the arms of God? "The suffering that unites us supremely with God by snatching us away from the world" (Teilhard de Chardin). When one is happy, it is very difficult not to just take God along "for the ride."

Today, since I have learned to live with my grief and consciously to accept separation from Oki as God's will, today I am grateful for the "aids our civilization offers," which now are not distractions but minor joys on my way to God.

The Secret Bond

Every four minutes a woman becomes a widow somewhere in this country — a grim statistic.

Between widows there is a remarkable bond; it is silently understood even between those who know each other slightly or not at all, for they bear the same sorrow.

The first time I went back to Mrs. V.'s antique store, she came up to me, having lost her own husband a few years before, and said simply, "Now you, too, are alone." The bond was forged.

Mrs. D. I had seen only on rare occasions; I thought of her as a cold businesswoman, driven by the goal of success. Once she took me home in her white Mercedes. She was wearing a provocative red hat, which I can still remember today because it stood in such contrast to what followed. As I said good-bye I mentioned her husband, who had died many years before. Gripping the steering wheel, she broke down and cried. An unsuspected contact was established, because there was now one point we had in common: we suffered.

It is also possible for an old friendship with a woman, who may have lost her husband years before, to turn into a new and deeper relationship when one becomes a widow. One word, and one realizes how the abyss opens at the feet of the other woman. It does not matter whether she is rich or poor, young or old, cultured or simple: experience of the same distress sets a bridge between two people, and one is no longer alone.

Pictures

Our pictures faded away in drawers; we had ourselves and did not need them. It was a motherly friend who got out the pictures of Oki and set them up, saying that he had been the head of the household and had a right to stand there.

At first I avoided looking at the pictures, from which Oki smiled at me with our lost joy, and sometimes I felt like tearing them up. Now I can bear them, for I think not only of the happiness that is past for us but also of the fulfillment of the promise that lies before us. But I am not much attached to these pictures; they show me Oki as he was, not as he is now in his other form of existence. I know that he is secure in God's protection between a miracle and a mystery: his spirit took on flesh at his birth, and put it off at death. Today as in the time of Solomon, to seek to understand this process of change and transformation would be a "striving after wind."

The Hotel Room

The hotel room in which I lay was like a bad dream: high, dirty walls, a light bulb in the ceiling, a crooked iron bed, the window opening on a stifling light shaft. Driving past to see me on the way to Italy, Carola had simply taken me along, and when night fell we turned off somewhere from the Strada del Sole. Vacation with Oki — that had once been to me a magic word of joy; it had meant being with him, free from the pressures of household and job. Without him, Sundays were all I needed; when one is alone, one does not exert oneself much, and being free for oneself is anything but happiness. I had not traveled except to visit friends. This was my first night alone in a hotel room. That time on the platform, today in this hotel room in an unknown town — two points at which I felt lost. Only that in a luxury hotel I would have been even lonelier, for I would not have been so dependent on God as in this bare ugliness.

Why did I feel desolate? Here in this iron bed in this rundown hotel I was no more lost than at home. My home only furnished the illusion of security. I was equally far from Oki and equally close to him wherever on earth I might be. And God was present everywhere.

The Etruscan Urns

Leaving Siena, Carola and I visited the Etruscan Museum at Volterra, with its thousands of funerary urns, carefully arranged according to the motifs of the reliefs. From the covers of the urns the dead sat upright and stared at me — thousands of the dead with disproportionately large heads and bizarrely foreshortened bodies. I walked in resignation from room to room until one motif caught my attention: "Farewell to the Departed." Family scenes were depicted: horror, resignation, hope, stark terror, despair — all the stages of separation by death; at the final parting, the emotions of all people of all ages are the same. The cover of one urn held me in its spell. It depicted an aged married couple, their large heads furrowed by the struggle of life, their foreshortened bodies slightly raised. In the way they inclined toward each other, in the way they looked at each other, there lay a silent familiarity and bond that death would never extinguish.

The Greeks thought of Death as the twin brother of Sleep, and depicted him as a handsome young boy with an extinguished torch. Why young? In the West, Death in the course of time became an old man of bones, a skeleton wielding his brutal scythe. Why old? Death — a devil? Should that which leads to God not be a beneficent spirit, tender, comforting? In the medieval fresco *The Triumph of Death* in the Campo Santo at Pisa, Death appears in the form he had among the Greeks, as an angel waving a still-burning torch, which he will soon extinguish for the happy company. How rarely Death appears as an angel in Christian art, how often he is the skeleton with the scythe! I have never understood what feelings lead men to personify death at all. For me death does not exist as an ugly skeleton or a handsome youth; for me there is only the dead body and the crossing of the spirit to God.

But this crossing, this mystery of God, a source of light to some and of terror to others, this mystery which dominates the life of believer and unbeliever alike from their first breath, will never be given form by an artist with all his means of expression. One can, however, depict the parting, the gap, the separation caused on earth by death through all the stages of despair, of hope, of anguish. That is what the Etruscans did in this motif, and that moved me, because it appeared true and natural to me.

Pushed Aside

At some time or other the departed one is pushed aside. With the passage of time he takes up less and less space. At first one needs only a pigeonhole and moves his papers aside a little; then one needs half a closet and sends his clothing to storage.

I pushed you aside because I wanted to be nearer to you, and it began when I decided to do my work in your room. On your desk were still lying things that you had used: your briefcase, the Chinese bowl holding the pencils, the pewter tray. At first I only removed the briefcase, in which you had kept the notes for your memoirs. Then I needed room for my articles and emptied the corner cupboard next to the desk.

And so I pushed you aside by wanting to be near you. That was the first step, and others followed; there were always reasons, minor, pitiful pretexts. No other man occupies your place, but you, now dead, are pushed aside. Each time I had a bad conscience, although my reason told me that it did not hurt you and that these rearrangements were matters of indifference. Rationalize as I might, it left a bad taste in my mouth and made me feel as though I had betrayed you.

I Can't Recall

Someday, perhaps, I shall no longer hear your singing, no longer see your smile, no longer feel your tenderness. Without giving it much thought I have lived with my memories as though it were the most natural thing in the world. The ability to remember I had not thought of as a gift, and now I am appalled at the thought that memory is a function of the brain, and as it fails I might lose you once more, this time in a fundamental way.

Why am I worried? I am on my way to that world where there will be no forgetting and losing!

Not to Call Him Back

Did I love less than Laodameia or Ricarda Huch? The one prayed so ardently for her lover, fallen at Troy, that he was allowed to return to her for a short time from the realm of the dead. To Ricarda Huch, the joy of Paradise would be nothing if she could be granted only an hour every hundred years to spend on earth with the man she loved, "an hour to take death's sleep from off us both, that we might recognize each other despite the power of death, and be inflamed once more with our old love."

No! Our body and our love is a stage that is past. I think of it constantly, but I do not want to taste again this happiness, which someday, when God will lead us to unimagined bliss, may seem a mere breath. To bring Oki back through my tears would prolong our way. I am impatient to evolve to the end that God wills. It is our calling to follow the departed, who are so much nearer to God than we are, not to call them back.

Rumors

"I do not fear death, but I am afraid of leaving Liliane alone" — words I found inscribed by Oki in his book of songs.

We are on the brink of war, people think. Many are packing their bags, many are stocking up on provisions, anyone who owns property is worried. There is nothing I need to rescue, and I need not worry about Oki. But in the midst of the panicky throng I suddenly feel lost, as I did upon that platform and in that hotel room. And once again I learn: the lonelier I am, the nearer to me God is. There is no place of security on earth; war, disease, old age, death, will always terrify us. Always and everywhere I am dependent on God's grace, in which I am always and everywhere secure.

Oki need not have worried about me, but that he did is a source of comfort.

In the End?

Does this small book mean that I want to *know*, where God has commanded us to have *faith*? In an article by Max Seckler I read of a professor of theology who, having spent his life teaching, retired from work and then began to take a personal interest in death and the beyond, subjects that previously had not been his specialty. He wanted to know where he was going. But after years of study he cast all his books aside and determined that he would take the last step in ignorance. He did so in ignorance and, as it is said, in faith. Is it not true that faith is strengthened in this very soil of ignorance, and in fact can flourish *only* there?

"Christianity is not a matter of science but of conscience, not of rational comprehension but of inner experience" (Melanchthon).

Death Is a Beginning

What is the meaning of life? I wanted to know that when I was seventeen years old. I imagine that all young people ask that question once in their lives, or if they do not put it so concretely, at least probe unconsciously for an answer. When I was seventeen I could not find the answer, but today it seems very simple to me: to mature into ripeness for God. All joys and all sorrows lead to God, the sorrows of death more than any other experience. The joy of my life, my marriage with Oki, was transformed into sorrow for his death. But my faith that I would someday, like Oki, be called to God's kingdom transformed this sorrow into joy.

Now I live with death, not with horrible loathing, but using it as a criterion to determine what is important, what unimportant in my life; as a stimulus to cheerfulness, for through it I shall recover those I love; and as a way of giving meaning to my work, since my efforts, no matter how minor and unimportant, may serve God's final goal.

"If we have faith, then everything about us begins to gleam" (Teilhard de Chardin). Even death gleams. For Oki it was a beginning, and for me, too, it will be a beginning. In the hospital room, in the bed behind my mother's, I saw five old women die in a single year, wretched, hopeless cases. Death is unimportant there, because it is part of the schedule.

Physical pain can be horrible, but not death. As among the monks of Mount Athos, it seemed to me in the hospital to be a symbol of emptiness. Whoever lives much with death or thinks much of it comes to realize its remarkable unimportance, its importance only as a beginning in another realm of God.

I am on my way to the realm where Jesus prepared a place for Oki, and where he will also prepare a place for me — how could I be without joy?

In his hymnal, Oki wrote a variation of Paul Gerhardt's jewel:

O sacred head, sore wounded, you have yet prevailed.
The pangs of death await — to bring us to God's eternity!

Through all distress I win the joy that awaits each new day that God accords me. Death is only one step following a million others, but it is the step that will take me from hope in God to assurance.